Aristotle and logical theory

JONATHAN LEAR

Professor of Philosophy
Yale University

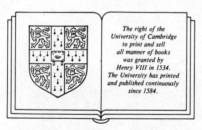

The right of the
University of Cambridge
to print and sell
all manner of books
was granted by
Henry VIII in 1534.
The University has printed
and published continuously
since 1584.

CAMBRIDGE UNIVERSITY PRESS

Cambridge
New York   Port Chester
Melbourne   Sydney

Published by the Press Syndicate of the University of Cambridge
The Pitt Building, Trumpington Street, Cambridge CB2 1RP
40 West 20th Street, New York, NY 10011, USA
10 Stamford Road, Oakleigh, Melbourne 3166, Australia

First published 1980
Reprinted 1985, 1988, 1990

Printed in Great Britain by
Woolnough Bookbinding Ltd, Irthlingborough, Northants.

Library of Congress Cataloguing in Publication Data
Lear, Jonathan.
Aristotle and logical theory.
Based on the author's thesis, Rockefeller University.
Includes index.
1. Aristotles – Logic. 2. Logic – History.
I. Title.
B491.L8L38   1980   160'.92'4   79-20273
ISBN 0 521 23031 4   hardback
ISBN 0 521 31178 0   paperback

Aristotle and logical theory

To Timothy Smiley

Contents

'Settle thy studies, Faustus, and begin
To sound the depth of that thou wilt profess;
Having commenc'd, be a divine in show,
Yet level at the end of every art,
And live and die in Aristotle's works.
Sweet Analytics, 'tis thou hast ravish'd me!'
                    Christopher Marlowe's Dr Faustus

Preface

'Logic is an old subject and since 1879 it has been a great one.'

W. V. O. Quine

Logic is an old subject and since the fourth century B.C. it has been a great one. Owing to the tremendous advances in logic since Frege's publication of the *Begriffsschrift* in 1879, philosophers have tended to ignore Aristotle's logic. They believe that Aristotle's syllogistic is a trivial logical system of little philosophical use. The syllogistic is not sufficiently sophisticated to express a single mathematically interesting proof, but philosophers rarely use any formal system actually to carry out a proof. Rather they make the logical system itself an object of study in order to gain insight into the nature of logical consequence, valid inference and proof. If one wishes to study the valid inferences that occur in mathematical arguments, it is, of course, important to have a logical system in which such arguments *could* be formalized. The syllogistic fails this requirement, but Aristotle did not think so. In *Prior Analytics* A23 and A25 he argues that every deductive argument can be expressed as a series of syllogistic inferences. That the argument is unconvincing masks the fact that simply by raising the problem, Aristotle earns the right to be considered not only the father of logic, but also the (grand)father of metalogic.

The very possibility of proof-theoretic inquiry emerges with Aristotle, for such study requires that one have a system of formal inferences that can be subjected to mathematical scrutiny. Before the syllogistic there was no such formalization that could be a candidate for proof-theoretic investigation. Aristotle thus opened a new realm of thought and discourse: he and his successors are able to answer questions about the nature of logical consequence and proof that could not even be posed by his predecessors.

In this book I offer an interpretation of Aristotle's logical programme; a programme which I believe to be one of the great triumphs of human thought. My hope is that the reader will come to see Aristotle as a philosopher of logic who is still worth thinking about and arguing with. This book was written with the student of the philosophy of logic in mind. Thus I have assumed no background knowledge of

Aristotle, but I have assumed that the reader has a minimal acquaintance with logic. However, I have tried to assume as little as possible, so that this book will be accessible to someone who is primarily interested in Aristotle.

I have relied on the Oxford Classical Texts of Aristotle's works. For quotations I have relied wherever possible on the Clarendon Aristotle Series,[1] making emendations when I thought they improved the sense of the text. Substantial changes are footnoted. The *Prior Analytics* has not yet been translated in the Clarendon Aristotle Series and the standard Oxford translation[2] often deviates from the Greek text, so I have often had to supply my own translation. Still I have tried to conform as much as possible to the Oxford translation. I am grateful to G. E. R. Lloyd for reviewing all of my translations. Of course, only I can be held responsible for their shortcomings. Indeed I am not thoroughly happy with all of the translations I left intact; but it seemed preferable, for the most part, to adopt the standard translations for certain words and phrases. For those who do not read Greek there will at least be some uniformity between commentaries and translations; those who do read Greek will know what the translations are translations of.

I have used the natural deduction formalization of Aristotle's logic given by Smiley and Corcoran.[3] '*Abd*' is read either as '*All b's are d*' or as '*d belongs to all b*'. '*Ebd*' is read either as '*No b's are d*' or as '*d belongs to no b*'. '*Ibd*' is read as '*Some b's are d*' or as '*d belongs to some b*'. '*Obd*' is read as '*Not all b's are d*' or as '*d does not belong to some b*'. For a class-theoretic interpretation, let the terms *a, b, c, d. . .* range over non-empty classes and let *A, E, I, O* stand, respectively, for class-inclusion, exclusion, overlap and non-inclusion.

This work began as a PhD thesis for The Rockefeller University. I would like to thank my thesis advisor Saul Kripke: whether we were pacing along First Avenue in New York or along Christ Church Meadows, Kripke was a source of stimulation and a model of intellectual clarity. From G. E. L. Owen I gained a deep respect for the ancient texts and a conviction that studying Aristotle can bring general philosophical enlightenment. Over the years I have had the pleasure of dis-

---

[1] Jonathan Barnes, *Aristotle's Posterior Analytics*; J. L. Ackrill, *Aristotle's Categories and De Interpretatione*; Christopher Kirwan, *Aristotle's Metaphysics, Books Γ, Δ, E*.
[2] G. R. G. Mure (translator), *Analytica Priora*, in W. D. Ross (ed.), *The Works of Aristotle Translated into English*.
[3] T. J. Smiley, 'What is a syllogism?', J. Corcoran, 'Aristotle's natural deduction system'.

cussing problems in the philosophy of logic with Paul Benacerraf and Donald Martin and general problems in philosophy with Bernard Williams. It was Williams who suggested I prepare my thesis for publication. Cynthia Farrar was an indefatigable editor of the penultimate draft, which was no small accomplishment considering she had mononucleosis at the time. She not only ruthlessly pursued split infinitives, she convinced me there was reason not to split them. Penny Thomson prepared an immaculate typescript.

I would like to thank the Master and Fellows of Trinity Hall, Cambridge, for electing me to a Research Fellowship, thus providing me with the time to prepare my thesis for publication.

I derived great sustenance while writing my thesis from the love and support of various friends and family: John Dunn, Judy Dunn, Cynthia Farrar, Harry Frankfurt, Tammy Jacoby, Susan James, Judy Lear, Martha Lear, Norman and Frances Lear, Ruth Marcus, Svetlana Mojsov, Ruth Morse and Stefan Collini, Charles Parkin, Quentin Skinner and Jonathan Spence.

My greatest intellectual debt is to Timothy Smiley. Attending his lectures on logic as a student at Clare College, Cambridge, I first conceived an interest in the field; it was he who suggested I take Aristotle seriously. Later, as a Fellow of Trinity Hall, I had the privilege of talking about Aristotle's logic during daily runs with Smiley: it was the most enjoyable way I have yet found of getting through five miles.

Throughout the period I was a graduate student my father, Harold Lear, was dying. My most vivid memory of Rockefeller is of taking daily walks across the street to New York Hospital to sit by his bedside and talk to him – about Aristotle, the Middle East, people and their feelings. For me, this book is a very small celebration of that joyous man.

May 1979   J.L.

I

Syllogistic consequence

The first sentence of the *Prior Analytics* states that the subject of inquiry is proof. However, Aristotle first presents his theory of the syllogism because, he says, it is more general: every proof is a syllogism, but not every syllogism is a proof (*An. Pr.* 25b28–31). Aristotle defines a syllogism as a '*logos* in which, certain things being posited, something other than what is posited follows of necessity from their being so' (*An. Pr.* 24b18ff).[1] What is it to follow of necessity? And how does Aristotle show that, given certain premisses, a conclusion follows of necessity? This chapter provides an introduction to Aristotle's logical programme.

The modern logician works with two notions of logical consequence. One is semantic: the logician provides an analysis of what it is for an arbitrary sentence to be true in a model. Then a sentence P is said to be a semantic consequence of a set of sentences X if P is true in every model in which all the members of X are true.[2] This semantic definition of consequence provides an analysis of what we mean by saying that P is a logical consequence of X if *whenever* all the members of X are true, P *must* be true. That is, it provides an analysis of what it is for a sentence to follow of necessity from other sentences. The other notion of consequence is syntactic. The logician specifies effective rules for manipulating symbols of a language and P is said to be a syntactic consequence of a set of sentences X if one can move from X to P using only the specified rules. Of course, the syntactic rules are chosen with the intention that the rules will at least preserve and if possible capture the relation of semantic consequence. In modern logic one proves formal inferences sound with respect to a semantics. From a modern

---

[1] The usual translations of *logos* in this context, e.g. 'discourse', 'argument', are not adequate. 'Discourse' may suggest dialogue or conversation which should not be present, 'argument' may suggest argumentative force which a syllogism need not possess (see Chapter 3 below). The problem of translating *logos* is of course not new. Says Goethe's Faust: 'I feel that I must open the fundamental text: must try, with honest feeling, to set down in my own beloved German that sacred original. It is written: "In the beginning was the Word!" Already I have to stop! Who will help me on? It's impossible to put such trust in the Word! I must translate some other way if I am truly enlightened by the spirit.'

[2] See Tarski, 'On the concept of logical consequence'.

perspective, it is a soundness proof which justifies a particular syntactic inference.[3]

However, it has become too easy to assume that a syntactic inference *must* be justified by some form of semantical soundness proof. This is because logicians have tended to treat formal systems as uninterpreted, as a safeguard against theoretical assumptions remaining hidden in the underlying logic.[4] The syntactical relation of formal deducibility is then defined as a relation between uninterpreted symbols of a formal language. The definition of such a relation depends upon an antecedent analysis of logical consequence, such as Tarski's, but, taken strictly as a relation among uninterpreted symbols, it is not a *consequence* relation at all. A syntactical relation, however, need not be restricted to uninterpreted symbols of a formal language. Of course, one must be able to determine whether a finite string of symbols is a formal derivation without recourse to their interpretation. One may nevertheless regard the rules of inference and deducibility relation as holding among interpreted sentences. In so far as the syntactic relation is genuinely one of consequence, it must contain a semantic ingredient.

To understand Aristotle's logical programme, it is crucial to distinguish a syntactic relation from a relation between uninterpreted symbols. For if one conflates 'syntactic' with 'uninterpreted', it seems one must provide a semantic analysis of consequence which the syntactic relation is supposed to capture. Aristotle does not offer a definition of 'following from necessity' and then show that the syllogisms are true to it. Rather he begins by presenting a few obviously valid inferences and invites one to agree that these are cases in which the conclusion follows of necessity from the premises. The syllogisms of the first figure –

$Aab\ Abc$	$Aab\ Ebc$	$Iab\ Abc$	$Iab\ Ebc$
Aac	Eac	Iac	Oac

– are said to be perfect (*An. Pr.* 25b32ff). A syllogism is *perfect* if it needs nothing other than what is stated to make evident what necessarily follows (*An. Pr.* 24b22–25). Hence to establish that the conclusion of a perfect syllogism follows from the premises, one should need to do no more than state the syllogism itself. For first figure syllogisms, this is virtually all that Aristotle does (cf. *An. Pr.* 25b37–26a2; 26a23–27).

---

[3] See Dummett, 'The justification of deduction'.

[4] For example Kleene says, 'First the formal system itself must be described and investigated by finitary methods and *without making use of an interpretation of the system*' (my emphasis). *Introduction to Metamathematics*, p. 69.

At *Prior Analytics* 26b29 he simply states that it is evident that the first figure syllogisms are perfect. No argument is given for their validity. For if the syllogisms are perfect, no argument need be given. Aristotle also introduces three rules of conversion:

From *Eba* infer *Eab*
From *Aba* infer *Iab*
From *Iba* infer *Iab*

He presents them as follows:

'In universal belonging it is necessary that the terms of the negative premiss should be convertible, e.g. if no pleasure is good, then no good will be pleasure; the terms of the affirmative must be convertible, not however universally, but in part [i.e. to a particular proposition], e.g. if every pleasure is good some good must be pleasure; in particular belonging, the affirmative must convert in part (for if some pleasure is good, then some good will be pleasure); but the negative need not convert, for if some animal is not a man, it does not follow that some man is not an animal.' (*An. Pr.* 25a5–13)

'First then, take a universal negative with the premiss *ab* [*Eba*]. If *a* belongs to no *b*, neither will *b* belong to any *a*. For if *b* belonged to some *a*, for example to *c*, it will not be true that *a* belongs to no *b*; for *c* is a *b*. But if *a* belongs to every *b*, then *b* will belong to some *a*. For if *b* belonged to no *a*, neither will *a* belong to any *b*: but it was assumed that *a* belongs to all *b*. Similarly too if the premiss is particular. For if *a* belongs to some *b*, then necessarily *b* belongs to some *a*: for if *b* belonged to no *a*, neither would *a* belong to any *b*. But if *a* does not belong to some *b*, it is not necessary that *b* does not belong to some *a*, e.g. if *b* is animal and *a* is man. Man does not belong to all animal, but animal belongs to all man.' (*An. Pr.* 25a14–26)

The point of Aristotle's argument is to get one to recognize these inferences not merely as valid, but as obviously valid. The passage 25a5–13 illustrates the three rules of conversion using the terms 'pleasure' and 'good'. The intention is that one simply see that the rules of conversion are true for these examples and that the examples are illustrative of valid rules. It would, of course, be a mistake to interpret 25a5–13 as offering a proof of the rules of conversion, for invalid inference patterns may have particular instances in which the premisses and conclusion are true. Consider, for example, 'if some pleasure is not good, some good will not be pleasure, therefore the terms of the particular *Oca* must convert'. Even if some good is not pleasurable and some pleasure is not good, this does not justify the convertibility of the particular negative premiss in general. One does not know that one has taken arbitrary terms, terms that are genuinely illustrative of a valid inference pattern, unless one knows that the inference pattern they illustrate is valid. But one *can* recognize Aristotle's examples as instances of valid inferences and that is because the inferences they illustrate are obviously valid.

Similarly, the argument which follows in 25a14–26 should not be viewed as a proof of the rules of conversion from principles which are logically or epistemically prior. In this passage Aristotle introduces term variables which transcend the problem of knowing that particular terms (e.g. 'good', 'pleasure') are genuinely arbitrary and illustrative of a valid inference. He also employs both *ekthesis* and argument by *reductio ad absurdum*. *Ekthesis* occurs in the step:

'For if *b* belonged to some *a*, for example to *c*, it will not be true that *a* belongs to no *b*; for *c* is a *b*.' (*An. Pr.* 25a16)

In my opinion, *ekthesis* is similar to the use of free variables in modern systems of natural deduction. Having assumed that some *a*'s are *b*, we are allowed to select an arbitrary particular instance of *a*, which is *b*. This corresponds to existential instantiation in natural deduction. So *c* should not be seen as another term variable like *a* and *b*, but as an arbitrary instance of an *a*. This view is not uncontentious:[5] others believe that *c* should be interpreted as a term variable having as an extension those *a*'s that are *b*. Whichever view of *ekthesis* is correct, the important point for the thesis I am advancing is that one not take Aristotle to be giving a proof of the rules of conversion according to any logically or epistemologically prior technique. The argument is designed solely to display the obviousness of the validity of the rules of conversion. Consider, by way of analogy, the modern rule of and-introduction: 'From *P* and *Q*, infer *P-and-Q*.' One would expect that anyone who understood conjunction would simply see that this inference is valid. No proof of validity could employ rules more evidently valid than this. Still, to make the obviousness of the inference apparent, one might argue 'Suppose *P* and *Q* but not *P-and-Q*. If not *P-and-Q* then either not *P* or not *Q*, but that is absurd, since one has *P* and *Q*.'

[5] Cf. e.g. Łukasiewicz, *Aristotle's Syllogistic From the Standpoint of Modern Formal Logic*, pp. 59–67; Patzig, *Aristotle's Theory of the Syllogism*, pp. 156–68; Kneale, *The Development of Logic*, p. 77.

This is not a proof of and-introduction from logically prior rules or principles: no such proof is needed. With an apparently obvious inference, a doubt may remain whether something has been overlooked, whether one has fully understood the inference. The direct derivation of an absurdity from supposing the inference invalid reveals that the appearance of obviousness is genuine.

A syllogism is *imperfect* if it needs additional propositions set out, which are necessary consequences of the premisses, in order to make it evident that the conclusion follows from the premisses (*An. Pr.* 24b24). Patzig has noted that this definition presupposes that all imperfect syllogisms can be perfected.[6] Aristotle does not admit a category of unobvious syllogisms *per se*: syllogisms are divided exhaustively into those that are obvious and those that can be made obvious. The perfection of an imperfect syllogism '*P, Q* so *R*' consists in showing how one can move from the premisses *P* and *Q* to the conclusion *R* using the rules of conversion and first figure inferences (*An. Pr.* A5, 6). An example is the perfection of *Cesare*, '*Enm, Aom* so *Eon*', in the second figure:

Since *Enm*, by conversion, *Emn*; but since *Aom* one can form the perfect first figure syllogism *Celarent* '*Emn, Aom* so *Eon*' (cf. *An. Pr.* 27a3ff).

Aristotle's strategy is to isolate a handful of obviously valid inferences and justify the remaining inferences by showing that they are redundant: one can move from premisses to conclusion without them. In the three figures Aristotle considers 48 possible pairs of premisses. Aside from the perfect first figure syllogisms, he is able to eliminate by counterexample all but ten other premiss-pairs as having no syllogistic consequences.[7] The remaining ten syllogisms can be perfected: they can, in Aristotle's words, be *reduced* to first figure syllogisms (*An. Pr.* 29b1).

Such a strategy demands a flexible conception of the means of perfection. Most notably, the moods *Baroco* ('*Acb, Oab* so *Oac*') and *Bocardo* ('*Obc, Aba* so *Oac*') are perfected by *reductio ad absurdum* arguments (*An. Pr.* 27a36, 28b17).[8] The problem with these syllogisms

---

[6] Patzig, *Aristotle's Theory of the Syllogism*, p. 45.

[7] See Chapter 4.

[8] One must be careful to distinguish the reduction of one syllogism to another, which uses a *reductio ad absurdum* argument, from a *per impossibile* syllogism. See e.g. Kneale, *The Development of Logic*, pp. 76–9; Patzig, *Aristotle's Theory of the Syllogism*, pp. 144–56. *Per impossibile* syllogisms are discussed in Chapter 3.

is that since the particular negative premiss does not convert, the only possible conversion that can be applied is one from the universal affirmative premiss to a particular affirmative premiss. For example, with *Baroco*, the only valid conversion possible is from *Acb* to *Ibc*. This leaves two particular premisses – *Ibc*, *Oab* – and there is no perfect inference with two particular premisses.[9] Aristotle is thus forced to abandon the direct method of perfection he has been using. To derive the conclusion *Oac*, he assumes its contradictory *Aac* and then infers, by the perfect first figure syllogism *Barbara*, an impossible conclusion:

> Suppose *Aac*, then since *Acb* it follows that *Aab*; but that is impossible since *Oab*; therefore *Oac*.

The claim that for any imperfect syllogism '*P, Q* so *R*' one can prove *R* from *P* and *Q* using only perfect inferences must therefore be treated with caution: it is true only if we are willing to countenance certain deviant means of perfection that are needed to make the claim true. The value of the doctrine of perfection – that all syllogisms are exhaustively partitioned into those that are perfect and those that can be made perfect – is that Aristotle is able to present a coherent logical theory without giving an analysis of the concept of logical consequence. For perfect syllogisms one can simply point to their validity; for imperfect syllogisms one justifies them by showing how they can be perfected.

The debate that has ensued since Aristotle's time over the obviousness of perfect syllogisms has focused on two related issues: (1) What is it about the perfect syllogisms that makes their validity evident? (2) What is it about the imperfect syllogisms that makes them less evidently valid than perfect syllogisms?

Kneale has suggested that in first figure syllogisms the terms are arranged so that the transitivity of the relations 'belongs to' and 'is predicated of' is evident.[10] Kneale notes that Aristotle presents two distinct formulations of a first figure syllogism. One formulation talks of one term being in another as in a whole (25b31); the other talks of one term being predicated of all of another (25b37ff).

> 'Whenever three terms are so related to one another that the last is in the middle as in a whole, and the middle is either in, or excluded

---

[9] Indeed there is no formally valid syllogistic inference at all with two particular premisses.
[10] Kneale, *The Development of Logic*, p. 73.

from, the first as in or from a whole, the extremes must be related by a perfect syllogism . . . If *a* is predicated of all *b* and *b* of all *c*, *a* must be predicated of all *c* . . .' (*An. Pr.* 25b31–39)

In these formulations, Aristotle reverses the order in which the terms are presented, thus preserving the obviousness of the transitivity of each relation. If this analysis of why Aristotle called the first figure syllogisms perfect is correct, then, as Patzig has said, the debate over what makes perfect syllogisms perfect has occurred in a misleading context.[11] For the traditional formulation of a syllogistic premiss 'All *a*'s are *b*'s' rather than the Aristotelian '*b* is predicated of all *a*' or '*b* belongs to all *a*', in conjunction with the presentation of the syllogistic premisses in the same order as Aristotle presented them, destroys the very feature of the first figure inferences that is supposed to make them perfect.

What I should like to argue, however, is that these questions – of what it is that makes first figure syllogisms perfect and whether or not the second and third figure syllogisms are less obviously valid – though of interest in themselves, are irrelevant to the development of Aristotle's logical programme. All that is crucial to his programme is that there be agreement *that* the first figure syllogisms are obviously valid. One need not know why. If Aristotle was unable to provide an explicit analysis of the relation 'follows of necessity', and took it as primitive, he may equally well have been unable to articulate what it is to follow obviously of necessity. Further, Aristotle is far less committed to the unobviousness of the imperfect syllogisms than he is to the obviousness of the first figure syllogisms. For the first figure syllogisms form the basis of a logical programme that is carried out in the absence of an analysis of the concept of syllogistic consequence.

Because Aristotle did not offer an analysis of 'follows of necessity' there is an indeterminacy in the strength of this consequence relation. This is reflected in the fact that for any terms *a*, *b*, *c* '*Aab* & *Abc* ⊃ *Aac*' will be true if and only if in every interpretation in which *Aab* and *Abc* are both true, *Aac* will be true. A similar situation holds for every valid syllogistic inference. Thus, for every syllogism, the syllogism will preserve truth for any substitution of terms in the language if and only if in every interpretation in which the premisses are true, the conclusion is true. It would be anachronistic to ascribe to Aristotle a modern conception of semantic consequence: the concept of a language

[11] Patzig, *Aristotle's Theory of the Syllogism*, pp. 57–61.

having various interpretations is too recent and hard-won a discovery. Rather, Aristotle is working with the presemantic idea of interpretation by replacement: a statement-form is seen to have various instances. One obtains an interpretation of a syllogistic formula by substituting specific terms, of the appropriate logical category, for the schematic letters. Every syllogistic inference is *valid under replacement* in that for every substitution of terms which makes the premisses true, the conclusion is true.[12] This, however, only sets a lower bound on the strength of the syllogistic consequence relation. One cannot recover the precise strength of the relation of following of necessity.

Why was Aristotle able to take 'follows of necessity' as a primitive notion? One trivial reason is that there is a sufficient variety of Greek common nouns. When Aristotle wishes to show, for example, that the rule of conversion 'From *Oac* infer *Oca*' is invalid, he uses the terms 'animal' and 'man' (*An. Pr.* 25a12, 25a22ff). Not all animals are men, but it does not follow that not all men are animals. To show the validity of the other rules of conversion, Aristotle used the terms 'pleasure' and 'good'. These terms are inappropriate to reveal the invalidity of 'From *Oac* infer *Oca*' because, arguably, some pleasure is not good and some good is not pleasurable. Imagine for a moment that all common nouns in Greek happened to be such that if *Oac* is true, then *Oca* is true. Aristotle would have had to resort to some form of semantical argument by interpretation if he were to establish the invalidity of this inference. A more substantial reason is that Aristotle is willing to expand the means of perfection. Suppose, for example, that Aristotle was not acquainted either with argument by *reductio ad absurdum* or with *ekthesis*. A problem would then arise with the perfection of *Baroco* or *Bocardo*, for, as we have seen, neither can be perfected in the normal way, by a series of conversions. Because he is willing to countenance deviant methods of perfection, Aristotle is able to take 'follows of necessity' as a primitive. For he is able, by hook or by crook, to reduce the unobvious syllogisms to the obvious; and the obvious he is content to leave unexplained.

Whatever the strength of the consequence relation, a syllogism is something that has structure as well as semantic force. Łukasiewicz and, following him, Patzig, have argued that the syllogism is not an inference from premisses to conclusion, but a conditional in which the premisses function as a conjunctive antecedent and the conclusion as a

---

[12] For a discussion of validity under replacement, see Michael Dummett, *Elements of Intuitionism*, pp. 218ff.

consequent.[13] For example, the syllogistic mood *Barbara* is treated not as an inference, but as a single sentence 'If *Aab* and *Abc* then *Aac*.' This interpretation has already been seriously discredited by Smiley and Corcoran,[14] but it is nevertheless worthwhile for the present inquiry to see what is wrong with it. First, the opening sentence of the *Prior Analytics* states that the scope of inquiry is proof (24a10) and one cannot make sense of the claim that a proof is a type of syllogism (25b28ff) if one treats a syllogism as a conditional. A proof is an argument, with definite structure, from several sentences functioning as premises to a conclusion. It is not a single sentence. Second, Aristotle's distinction between direct and *per impossibile* syllogisms refers solely to the manner in which conclusions are derived. In a *per impossibile* syllogism Aristotle says that one supposes the contradictory of what one wishes to prove and then derives an admittedly false conclusion (*An. Pr.* 62b29–31; 41a23–24).[15] For example, to prove *Abd* one argues:

Suppose *Obd*, then since *Abc*, it follows that *Ocd*; but *Acd*; therefore *Abd*.

(The premises are in bold type.) Aristotle shows that the premises of this *per impossibile* syllogism provide the premises for a direct syllogism with the same conclusion:

$$\frac{Abc \ Acd}{Abd}$$

Aristotle shows that any conclusion that can be derived by a direct syllogism can also be derived, from the same premises, by a *per impossibile* syllogism. Conversely any conclusion that can be derived by a *per impossibile* syllogism can also be derived, from the same premises, by a direct syllogism (*An. Pr.* 45a26, 62b39; *An. Pr.* B11–14).[16] This distinction therefore requires that one attribute to the syllogism an argumentative structure which a conditional lacks.[17]

---

[13] Łukasiewicz, *Aristotle's Syllogistic*, pp. 20–30; Patzig, *Aristotle's Theory of the Syllogism*, pp. 3–4.

[14] Smiley, 'What is a syllogism?'; Corcoran, 'Aristotle's natural deduction system'.

[15] Clearly, Aristotle's *description* of a *per impossibile* syllogism differs from the traditional account of a *per impossibile* in which it is emphasized that one is deriving a contradiction from a supposition and a set of premises. Cf. J. N. Keynes, *Studies and Exercises in Formal Logic*, section 257. For a discussion of this see Chapter 3 below.

[16] See Chapter 3.

[17] Further, the evidence Łukasiewicz and Patzig adduce is unconvincing. The evidence consists in the presence of the Greek word for 'if' (εἰ) before a statement of the premises and the absence of the Greek word for 'therefore' (ἄρα) before the statement of the conclusion. However, that at a later time the word 'therefore' is conventionally used to mark that the conclusion of an inference is being drawn does not, of

A proof, for Aristotle, is a syllogism which enables one, simply by grasping it, to gain knowledge of the conclusion (*An. Pst.* 71b18ff). The premisses of a proof must possess certain important properties; for instance, they must be true, explanatory of, better known than and prior to the conclusion (*An. Pst.* 71b20). A syllogism in which the premisses had all the requisite properties would be a proof. It follows that a syllogism cannot merely consist in a relation of semantic consequence between premisses and conclusion. For if one simply states the axioms of a theory and a non-trivial semantic consequence *P*, there may be no way to tell whether *P* follows of necessity from the axioms. One cannot prove, for instance, that every triangle has interior angles equal to two right angles (Euclid 1–32) merely by stating Euclid's postulates and then the theorem. A proof has a structure which reveals that the conclusion must be true if the premisses are. Therefore a syllogism must have a structure such that if the premisses had the appropriate properties one would be able, simply by studying the syllogism, to see that the conclusion is true. Must not a proof be a perfect (or perfected) syllogism? Curiously Aristotle does not mention this when discussing the properties a syllogism must have to be a proof (cf. *An. Pst.* A2–33). The reason, I think, is because every imperfect syllogism is perfectible. Any imperfect syllogism already has a structure such that it is possible to interpolate intermediate deductive steps designed to make it evident that the conclusion is a consequence of the premisses.

A syllogism should thus be thought of as a deduction, an entity which possesses a structural as well as a semantic relation between premisses and conclusion. Aristotle's project is to provide a formal analysis of the non-formal deductions with which he was familiar. Indeed, there is an ambiguity in Aristotle's use of the word 'syllogism' similar to that in the modern use of the word 'deduction'. There is, first, the use of 'syllogism' in the broad sense of the definition as a *logos* in which, certain things being posited, something other than what is

---

course, imply that at a period before the convention is in use the absence of 'therefore' should be taken as evidence that an inference is not being made. Further, there is no need to take 'if' (εἰ) as the hallmark of a conditional: it could equally well signify that the premisses are to be supposed or entertained. Even in contemporary English, the use of 'If . . . then . . .' is neither criterion that one has stated a conditional nor that one has not drawn an inference. If one were actually reasoning validly, rather than remarking on the validity of an inference, the use of 'If . . . then . . .' would not be unnatural. Whether or not the statement should be interpreted as a conditional or an inference would depend upon the context of utterance and not merely on that particular mode of expression. For a development of this and other criticisms of Łukasiewicz, see Smiley, 'What is a syllogism?'.

posited follows of necessity from their being so (*An. Pr.* 24b18). This corresponds to our use of 'deduction' in the general sense of an informal argument in which the conclusion is a logical consequence of the premisses. There is, in particular, no reference to the number of premisses, the number of inferences or their form. Second, there is the use of 'syllogism' in the narrow sense, used to describe the formal inferences and chains of formal inferences that Aristotle isolated. In a similar fashion, we use 'deduction' to refer to formal deductions of a particular logical system. This ambiguity is tolerable since the value of the formal syllogistic is supposed to derive from the fact that a syllogism in the broad sense can be represented as a syllogism or chain of syllogisms in the narrow sense.[18]

Aristotle's understanding of the syllogism is analogous to the modern logician's understanding of a computable function. The modern logician has an intuitive, perhaps vague, idea of what it is for a function to be computable. He also has a mathematically precise definition of a recursive function. Church's thesis, which asserts that the computable functions are the recursive functions, offers a mathematical analysis of the intuitive notion of computability. Similarly, Aristotle had an intuitive understanding of discourse in which certain things followed of necessity from others and, in *Prior Analytics* A4–6, he was able to isolate a mathematically precise system of formal inferences. In the beginning of *Prior Analytics* A4, Aristotle says that he can state how *all* syllogisms come to be (25b27). In *Prior Analytics* A23 he argues that all syllogisms without qualification come about through the three figures (40b20). This is not a claim that any logical consequence relation can be formalized as a syllogistic proof: for, unlike the modern logician, Aristotle is not working with two distinct conceptions of consequence, one semantic, one syntactic. To be a syllogism, even in the broad sense, is to have structure as well as to express a consequence relation. Rather, the claim is that any direct deductive argument can be expressed as a series of syllogistic inferences.[19] Aristotle is declaring that any non-formal deduction, such as the proof that a triangle has interior angles equal to two right angles, can be recast as a formal deduction. One might call this claim 'Aristotle's Thesis'.

Unlike Church's thesis, which is tested empirically by showing that

---

[18] I shall use 'syllogism' as Aristotle uses '$\sigma\upsilon\lambda\lambda o\gamma\iota\sigma\mu\acute{o}\varsigma$' and I shall reserve the word 'syllogistic' for cases in which I wish to speak specifically of the formal inferences in the three figures.

[19] Aristotle excepts hypothetical syllogisms; see Chapter 3.

particular functions recognized as computable are all recursive, Aristotle does not try to formalize particular deductions, but rather presents an abstract argument for his thesis. He assumes that the conclusion of every non-formal deductive argument – every syllogism in the broad sense – is essentially of the form of a syllogistic formula, i.e. *Abc*, *Ebc*, *Ibc* or *Obc*. He then argues proof-theoretically that the only way such a conclusion can be directly derived is through premisses which link the terms of the conclusion through a middle term relating them (*An. Pr.* 40b30–41a20). The ways in which the terms of the conclusion can be related by a middle term correspond, as Aristotle sees it, to the three figures (*An. Pr.* 41a14ff).

It is now easy to criticize the assumption that the conclusion of every deduction is in syllogistic form. Łukasiewicz and Mueller have argued that though Aristotle understood that the validity of an argument may depend on its form, he did not seriously consider how a particular deduction can be formalized.[20] Mueller argues that Aristotle's translation of non-formal statements into syllogistic formulas was so casual that he was not in a position to recognize that his favourite geometrical theorem – that a triangle has interior angles equal to two right angles (Euclid 1–32) – cannot be rendered as a syllogistic formula. The picture that emerges from the Łukasiewicz-Mueller critique is of an Aristotle concerned with formal validity, but not with formalization.

However, not all the evidence supports this view. In *Prior Analytics* A35, Aristotle warns one not to try always to set out syllogisms using particular terms:

'We must not always seek to set out the terms in a single name: for we shall often have complexes of words (λόγοι) to which a single name is not given. Hence it is difficult to reduce syllogisms with such terms. Sometimes too it will happen that one will be deceived because of such a search, e.g. the belief that syllogism can establish that which has no *middle*. Let *a* stand for two right angles, *b* for triangle, *c* for isosceles triangle. *a* then belongs to *c* because of *b*: but *a* belongs to *b* without the mediation of another term: for the triangle in virtue of its own nature contains two right angles, consequently there will be no middle term for the proposition *ab* though it is *provable*. For it is clear that the middle must not always be assumed to be a particular thing, but sometimes a complex of words, as happens in the case mentioned.' (*An. Pr.* 48a29–39)

[20] Łukasiewicz, *Aristotle's Syllogistic*, pp. 15–19; Mueller, 'Greek mathematics and Greek logic'.

This passage does not refute the Łukasiewicz–Mueller critique, but it does weaken it. It is true that Aristotle here allows that the conclusion of Euclid 1–32 has the form *Aba*. However, he specifically warns that one must not try to find a syllogistic proof of it, though he also admits that the conclusion is provable. His worry is precisely formalization. Though Aristotle does think that 'Every triangle has interior angles equal to two right angles' has the form of a syllogistic formula, he is not thereby led to believe that the proof of it is formalizable.

How is one to reconcile this passage with the argument of *Prior Analytics* A23? I do not believe there can be a reconciliation, for the tension that exists between these two is not superficial. At best one can hope to explain why this tension exists. I would like to offer the following conjectures: First, Aristotle shares with contemporary logicians a primary interest in metalogic. He uses the syllogistic as modern logicians use the predicate calculus; not as a tool with which one actually formalizes mathematical proofs, but rather as an object about which one can reason in order to gain insight into the structure of proof. In order to believe that the study of a particular formal system can shed light on the nature of proof, one must believe that proofs are formalizable within it. Aristotle differs from modern logicians in not having a system capable of formalizing mathematical proofs. However, it would be just as important to him as it is to modern logicians to have an argument to show that his formal system was adequate for the expression of proofs.

Second, if Aristotle is to present a unified and coherent logical theory without giving an analysis of the concept of following of necessity it is essential that all deductions, non-formal and formal, be systematically related to the perfect syllogistic inferences. Aristotle has provided (i) an analysis of the three syllogistic figures which reduces imperfect inferences to perfect ones; and (ii) an argument that the three syllogistic figures are adequate for the expression of all non-formal deductions. If that argument were valid, it would follow that any deductive consequence of any set of premisses can be reached by a series of obviously valid inferences. For any deduction could, in theory, be expressed as a chain of syllogistic inferences and those formal inferences could be perfected. In one's actual deductive practice one may move quickly, making large inferential steps with, perhaps, a passing reference to theorems already proved. But this practice is licensed, for Aristotle, not by an analysis of consequence, but by the guarantee that, in doubtful cases, any non-formal deduction can be formalized, and any formalized deduction can be perfected – transformed into an argument in which every step follows obviously.

Were this not thought to be possible, Aristotle would not have been able to take 'follows of necessity' as primitive and justify all deductive arguments by recourse to the obvious. He would have had to supply an analysis of the concept of syllogistic consequence and this, I believe, he was not in a position to do.

2

Completeness and compactness[1]

A logic is *complete* if given any logical consequence P of a set of premisses X, there is a formal deduction from X to P.[2] The completeness of a logic ensures that its proof procedure is adequate to reveal all logical consequences. A logic is *compact* if given that P is a logical consequence of X, then P is a logical consequence of some finite subset of X. If X is finite, then the subset may be X itself. The compactness of a logic is important in those cases in which X is infinite; since then a compactness theorem guarantees that a finite proper subset will logically imply P. This guarantee is crucial to the proof of completeness. A formal proof has only finitely many steps and each step has only finitely many premisses. Thus a proof can at best display a logical consequence of a finite set of premisses. If compactness fails, there is no hope of the logic being complete.

Since, as I argued in the previous chapter, Aristotle had a unified notion of logical consequence – not the bifurcated notion of semantic and syntactic consequence – the search for a completeness or compactness proof in the *Analytics* may appear paradoxical. For, from the perspective of modern logic, the point of a completeness theorem is to establish the extensional equivalence of two distinct consequence relations.[3] Further, consciousness of the distinction between syntactic and semantic consequence – and therefore of the need to prove completeness – is very recent. Although Frege respects the distinction between syntax and semantics, he is not explicitly aware of it.[4] It would be anachronistic to attribute to Aristotle the ability to raise the question of

---

[1] This chapter is a revised version of my article, 'Aristotle's compactness proof', which appeared in *The Journal of Philosophy*, 1979.

[2] Often a definition of completeness only requires that every valid formula be provable. In so far as a logician is primarily concerned with capturing the relation of logical consequence, such a definition is inadequate. See Dummett, *Frege: Philosophy of Language*, pp. 430–41.

[3] See Dummett, 'The justification of deduction'.

[4] See Dummett, *Frege: Philosophy of Language*, pp. 81–2. The development of an awareness that there is a problem of completeness has an interesting history. Though Skolem all but proved completeness – it is a trivial corollary of his 1922 theorem – he did not then even see it as a problem. See Wang, 'A survey of Skolem's works in logic'; Wang, *From Mathematics to Philosophy*, pp. 8–11.

completeness, which depends on an awareness of the syntax/semantics distinction.

Nevertheless, Aristotle is able to address a problem analogous to completeness. Let us say that the syllogistic is complete with respect to deduction if every deductive argument can be represented as a series of syllogistic inferences. Is the syllogistic complete with respect to deduction? Can every syllogism, in the broad sense of the term, be expressed as a series of syllogistic inferences? As mentioned in the last chapter, *Prior Analytics* A23 tries to offer an affirmative answer in a rather grand style. The conclusion of every deduction is assumed to have the form of a syllogistic formula and the deduction itself is said to link the terms of the conclusion in a way which corresponds to one of the three syllogistic figures.

In *Prior Analytics* A25 Aristotle argues that a deduction with an arbitrary finite number of premisses can be expressed as a series of two-premissed syllogistic inferences. Unfortunately, Aristotle begs the question by assuming that nothing follows from a set of premisses that does not follow when the premisses are taken a pair at a time.[5] However, he at least confronted the problem of deductions from an arbitrarily finite number of premisses; and in so doing he seems far more modern than those, following in the so-called Aristotelian tradition, who simply assumed a syllogism to have two premisses.

Could Aristotle have addressed a problem analogous to compactness? One might well be sceptical. For if one's understanding of consequence is tied to the notion of a deductive argument, it appears that one could only conceive of a sentence being a consequence of a finite number of premisses. To raise the question of compactness one must be able to envisage the possibility of a sentence being a logical consequence of an infinite number of premisses. This seems to require that one have an independent conception of semantic consequence. Without such a conception it seems that Aristotle would be forced to leave his completeness proof dangling with the case of deductions from arbitrarily finite numbers of premisses, denied even the opportunity to pose one of the most interesting problems in a completeness proof.

Such a pessimistic view is, however, unwarranted: Aristotle was not a prisoner of these conceptual constraints. The question of how many steps are required to prove a conclusion can be asked seriously only after one has a formal system, such as the syllogistic, in which to present proofs. The syllogistic requires that proofs be finitary. Since there are

[5] For a critique of this argument, see Smiley, 'What is a syllogism?'.

no infinitary rules of inference, there is no way to express within it a proof requiring infinitely many premisses. Does the finitary nature of syllogistic proofs impose any limitation on the formation of syllogisms? This problem, the analogue of compactness, arises within the theory of proof. Suppose one has a syllogistic proof in which not all the premisses are principles. For example, suppose one has the syllogism

$$\frac{Abc_0 \quad Ac_0 d}{Abd}$$

in which only the premiss Abc_0 is a principle. To try to prove the premiss $Ac_0 d$ one augments the syllogism:

$$\frac{Abc_0 \quad \dfrac{Ac_0 c_1 \quad Ac_1 d}{Ac_0 d}}{Abd}$$

If either of the premisses $Ac_0 c_1$ or $Ac_1 d$ is not a principle one continues this process by supplying a proof of it. This process terminates when all premisses of the syllogism are principles. In *Posterior Analytics* A19–22 Aristotle offers an analogue of a compactness proof. He argues that the process of improving a proof by providing proofs of all demonstrable premisses will always terminate after finitely many steps. It follows that the finitary nature of syllogistic proofs imposes no limit on the amount of knowledge that can be gained through proof.

Any genuinely infinite proof must include steps with infinitely many premisses. For, by König's lemma, any finitely-branching tree can have infinitely many nodes only if there is at least one infinite branch running through the tree. For example, in the syllogistic one could imagine a structure:

(π)

$Ac_0 c_1 \quad Ac_1 d$

$$\frac{Abc_0 \qquad\qquad Ac_0 d}{Abd}$$

where the nodes were syllogistic formulas and the formation

represented an immediate syllogistic inference. Now if there were infinitely many nodes above the conclusion *Abd*, then since every inference is from two premisses, there would have to be an infinite branch; in π it is symbolized as the right-hand branch. But then π could not be a proof. For a proof must begin from axioms or principles, and the infinite branch in the proof tree is an infinitely 'backwards running' series from the conclusion. As a proof, π could never get started. (In logician's terminology, a proof must form a sequence and the infinite branch provides an infinitely descending series, which is impossible by the definition of sequence.) Thus an infinite proof must be one with infinitary rules of inference.

Given the formal structure of the syllogistic, for there to be conclusions that would be demonstrable only if one countenanced infinitary proofs, there would have to be infinitely long chains of predication of certain sorts. Aristotle asks three questions about the nature of predication (*An. Pst.* 81b30–82a7).

(1) Can there be an infinite chain of predication 'ascending' from a fixed subject? Let *b* be a subject of predication that itself cannot be predicated of another subject. Suppose c_0 applies immediately to *b*. Might there not be an infinite series $c_0 c_1 \ldots$ such that for all *n*, c_{n+1} applies to c_n?

(2) Can there be an infinite chain of predication 'descending' from a fixed predicate? Suppose *b* is a predicate which is not the subject of any predication, but which applies immediately to c_0. Might there not be an infinite series $c_0 c_1 \ldots$ such that for all *n*, c_n applies immediately to c_{n+1}? The question is whether there is an infinitely descending chain of predication never terminating in an ultimate subject.

(3) Can there be an infinite number of middle terms between two fixed extremes?

Suppose that the answer to (1) were affirmative; i.e. that there was an infinitely long chain of predication $c_0 c_1 \ldots$ ascending from a fixed subject *b*. Given the appropriate principles, one could then prove Abc_1, $Abc_2 \ldots Abc_n \ldots$. For example,

$$\frac{Abc_0 \qquad Ac_0 c_1}{\dfrac{Abc_1 \qquad Ac_1 c_2}{Abc_2}}$$

In general, for any *n*, the proof that Abc_n would take only *n* steps. While there would be an infinite number of predicates for which it is possible to prove that b is the subject, each of the proofs would be of finite length.

An affirmative answer to (2) would create a situation symmetrical to that just described. Given principles of the form Ac_0b and $Ac_{n+1}c_n$, for any n one could prove Ac_nb. However, each such proof would be of finite length. For any n the proof that Ac_nb would require n steps.

Finally, suppose one could construct an infinitary proof. If one were to answer (3) affirmatively there might be conclusions which could be demonstrated from principles only through an infinite number of middle terms. Imagine, for example, a series $bc_0c_1 \ldots c_\omega d$. If one were to try to prove Abd, one would need some form of omega-rule of inference, e.g.

$$\frac{Abc_0 \quad Ac_0c_1 \ldots Ac_{n-1}c_n \ldots Ac_{\omega-1}c_\omega. \quad Ac_\omega d}{Abd}$$

A negative answer to (3) shows that even if one were to countenance infinitary proofs, there would be no new conclusions one could prove thereby. If there are only finitely many middle terms between any appropriate principles and conclusion, then an infinitary proof is not simply beyond our conceptual grasp or too complex for the formalism: it is unnecessary. Of course, Aristotle is not concerned with the possibility of infinitary proofs: he is trying to show that the process of proving demonstrable premisses will terminate after finitely many steps. His argument provides a fundamental test of the adequacy of the syllogistic.

Why should Aristotle have bothered with questions (1) and (2)? His strategy in *Posterior Analytics* A20 is to argue that negative answers to (1) and (2) entail a negative answer to (3). If the chains of predication ascending from a given subject or descending from a given predicate both terminate, then there cannot be an infinite number of middle terms.

'If d is predicated of b and the terms in between – the c's – are infinitely many, it is clear that it would be possible both that from d downwards one thing should be predicated of another *ad infinitum* (for before b is reached there are infinitely many terms in between), and that from b upwards there are infinitely many before d is reached. Hence if these things are impossible, it is also impossible for there to be infinitely many terms between d and b.' (*An. Pst.* 82a24–30)[6]

---

[6] I translate 'ἄπειρος' as 'infinite' rather than Barnes' 'indefinite'. While Barnes admirably wishes to stress Aristotle's conception of the infinite as potential, I think Aristotle's argument is clearer if one simply translates 'ἄπειρος' as 'infinite' and notes that Aristotle construes the infinite potentially.

If this passage simply asserted that if there are an infinite number of middle terms separating subject and predicate then one can make an infinite number of predications starting from the ultimate subject or ultimate predicate, the argument would be invalid. If there is an infinite series of middle terms $c_0 c_1 \ldots$ between b and d it does not follow that if one starts from b or from d there will be an infinite number of predications before one reaches the other term. Let the series of middle terms $c_0 c_1 \ldots$ form an omega sequence. In such a case if one starts from b and successively predicates middle terms of b, there will be an infinite number of predications before one reaches d. But if one starts from d and moves down the chain of middle terms one will predicate d only of a finite number of middle terms before one reaches b. Though there are an infinite number of middle terms, an infinite series of predications can occur in only one direction. As soon as one predicates d of any subject in the series, there will remain only a finite number of middle terms between that subject and the ultimate subject b. (This is because there is no subject to which d immediately belongs.) Similarly one could invert the sequence of middle terms $b \ldots c_n c_{n-1} \ldots c_0 d$, so that there would only be a finite number of predications from b to d yet an infinite number of predications from d to b.

One might think that the conception of there being infinitely many predications from b to d, but only finitely many from d back to b would appear paradoxical in the absence of Cantor's theory of transfinite well-orderings. Yet Aristotle's argument embodies an implicit understanding that the existence of an infinite number of middle terms is not in itself sufficient for there to be infinite chains of predication. Aristotle insists that a negative answer to (3) is implied by the *conjunction* of negative answers to (1) and (2). If an infinite number of predications in one direction implied there was an infinite number of predications in the other direction, one could validly argue that a negative answer to (3) was implied by a negative answer to (1) or a negative answer to (2). That Aristotle correctly demands a conjunction, not a disjunction, of negative answers is evidence that he did not think an infinite series in one direction implies an infinite series in the other.

The idea of a series of predications being infinite in one direction, but finite in the other, is now derived from and explained by Cantor's theory of transfinite orderings. Aristotle, interpreting statements about infinity potentially, rejected the concept of actual infinity.[7] Thus it might appear odd to ascribe to Aristotle a conception of the infinite

[7] See *Physics* Γ 6.

that is now associated with acceptance of the notion of the actual infinite. However, it is in fact quite natural both to conceive of infinity potentially and to hold that a series that is infinite in one direction need not be infinite in the other. If the infinite is construed potentially, then to say that one can assign a subject b to an infinite series of predicates $c_0 c_1 \ldots$ is to say that one can assign b to the predicates $c_0 c_1 \ldots$ without end. The process never terminates. Similarly, to say that one can predicate d of an infinite series of subjects $c_0 c_1 \ldots$ is to say that the process of predicating d of subjects will never terminate. Thus to envisage the possibility of there being infinitely many middle terms with it possible to make an infinite series of predications in only one direction, Aristotle would have had to conceive of a process which never terminates, but the inverse of which terminates after only finitely many steps. Aristotle knew of such a process: counting. The process of counting natural numbers never terminates, but at any point there are only finitely many steps back to 0.

Notice also that question (3) has a significantly different structure from questions (1) and (2). Question (3) does not ask whether there can be infinitely ascending and descending chains of predication. Rather it asks:

> 'Is it possible for the terms in between to be infinitely many if the extremes are determined? I mean, e.g., if d belongs to b and c is a middle term for them, but for c and d there are other [middle terms], and for these others, is it possible for *these* to go on *ad infinitum*, or impossible? This is the same as to inquire whether there is proof of everything or [whether some terms] are bounded by one another.' (*An. Pst.* 82a2–8)[8]

Given fixed extreme terms, an infinite series of middle terms must, for Aristotle, be dense. Why is this?

If one takes the infinite to be potential, then an infinite chain of predication would be thought of in terms of a never ending process of moving through the chain. As with the natural numbers, this is clearly possible even if all the terms in the chain are contiguous. If the infinite is interpreted actually, it is only when one has an infinite series of predications in both directions that contiguity must fail. Consider, for example, a chain of predication $b c_{-1} c_{-2} \ldots c_\omega \ldots c_2 c_1 d$. In such a series

---

[8] I translate '*ἀπόδειξις*' as 'proof' rather than 'demonstration'. The problem is not with the ancient Greek, but with modern English. 'Demonstration' is rarely used in discussing proofs and when used it often has a technical sense.

there are infinite chains of predication in both directions, but the series becomes dense by c_ω which has no immediate predecessors. (Such a series is *dense at a point* c_ω, in that, if from c_ω one selects any term c_j, there will always be middle terms c_i between c_ω and c_j.) However, interpreting the infinite potentially, it seems one could conceive of an infinite chain of predication in both directions without the failure of contiguity. One would only need to think of the process of assigning b to successive predicates and the process of predicating d of successive subjects never terminating. It is not obvious why one could not imagine the processes in both directions moving through contiguous terms without end. For no matter from which extreme term one began making predications, one would never reach the limit stage c_ω.

I think, however, that the Aristotelian conception of the infinite is such that if the two extremes of a series are fixed, the only way the series could be infinite is if the series becomes dense at some point between the two extremes. That is, if the extremes b and d are fixed, the series $bc_0 \ldots d$ can be infinite only if some segment of it $c_i \ldots c_j$ is *dense* in the sense that any two members of it are separated by another. (I.e. let $c_i < c_j$ when Ac_ic_j but not Ac_jc_i; then the segment $c_i \ldots c_j$ is dense if whenever $c_i < c_p < c_q < c_j$ there exists c_k such that $c_p < c_k < c_q$.) Aristotle's construal of the infinite as potential dictates such an interpretation. To say that a process will terminate is, for Aristotle, equivalent to saying that it will terminate after finitely many steps. The concept of a process terminating after infinitely many steps is one Aristotle would reject. He distinguished at least two distinct types of infinite process: (*a*) the process of addition, e.g. counting through the natural numbers; (*b*) the process of division, e.g. successively dividing the space between 0 and 1. If only one extreme term is fixed, one can imagine an infinite series of predications as a process of addition, moving through an unending series of contiguous terms. But if both extreme terms are fixed, then a limit is set for both processes of predication. That both processes of predication terminate in limits implies that Aristotle could not think of them in terms of addition. On Aristotle's conception of the infinite, it would be most natural to think of there being an infinite number of middle terms between two extremes as a process of division. Given middle terms c_i, c_j one can find middle terms c_k such that $c_i < c_k < c_j$.

Further, there are proof-theoretic reasons for taking an infinite series of middle terms between two fixed extremes to be dense. Consider an expanded proof in the favoured form *Barbara*:

$$Abc_3 \quad Ac_3c_1 \qquad Ac_1c_4 \quad Ac_4c_0 \qquad Ac_0c_5 \quad Ac_5c_2 \qquad Ac_2c_6 \quad Ac_6d \quad \text{(iv)}$$

$$\overline{Abc_1 \qquad\qquad Ac_1c_0 \qquad\qquad Ac_0c_2 \qquad\qquad Ac_2d} \quad \text{(iii)}$$

$$\overline{Abc_0 \qquad\qquad\qquad\qquad Ac_0d} \quad \text{(ii)}$$

$$\overline{Abd} \quad \text{(i)}$$

The conclusion *Abd* establishes the extremes of a chain of predication that is expanded by interpolation at every level as one moves up the proof tree. The form of the expansion is:

line (i): $<b, d>$

(ii): $<b, c_0, d>$

(iii): $<b, c_1, c_0, c_2, d>$

(iv): $<b, c_3, c_1, c_4, c_0, c_5, c_2, c_6, d>$

At every stage a new term is interposed between every term in the chain established by the preceding stage. Thus if each branch of the proof were infinitely long, the proof tree as a whole would form a dense linear chain of predication.

Given an extended proof in *Barbara*, two terms in the associated chain of predication would be contiguous only if some branch through the tree terminated after finitely many steps. If the chain of predication were discrete, all branches would be finite and so too would be the proof and the associated chain of predication. If there are an infinite number of terms between the two fixed extremes b, d established by such a proof, then though some of the terms may be contiguous, at some point the chain must become dense.

Aristotle says that asking whether there can be an infinite number of middle terms between two fixed extremes is the equivalent of inquiring 'do proofs proceed to infinity, i.e. is everything demonstrable?' (*An. Pst.* 82a7). To claim that everything is demonstrable is, I think, to claim that in an attempted proof one never reaches principles. Given any premiss it can be derived from other premisses. This is precisely the situation that would arise if the series of middle terms were dense. Suppose one had a proof of *Abd* that moved through a dense series of middle terms $<c_i>$. Consider any premiss in the proof Ac_ic_j. This premiss could not be a principle because for any c_i, c_j there are $<c_k>$ $(i<k<j)$, such that $<c_k>$ stand as middle terms between c_i and c_j. With premisses that connect the extreme terms the situation is the same. Given a premiss of the form Abc_i there are $<c_k>$ such that $k<i$ through which c_i applies to b. With a proof of the form:

$$Abc_i \quad Ac_ic_j$$
$$\overline{Abc_j}$$

one could always expand it by deriving both of the premisses:

$$\frac{Abc_k \quad Ac_kc_i}{Abc_i} \qquad \frac{Ac_ic_n \quad Ac_nc_j}{Ac_ic_j}$$

$$Abc_j$$

These newly introduced premisses can themselves be derived.

It is *only* when the series of middle terms is dense that everything is demonstrable. If one had a sequence $bc_{-1}c_{-2} \ldots c_\omega \ldots c_2c_1d$ (which is *dense at a point c_ω*), there would be infinite chains of predication in both directions, but not every premiss could be derived from other premisses. Even if one were to have a proof of *Abd*, and even if the proof were infinitary, there would have to be some premisses of the form Ac_ic_j that could not be derived from other premisses. For there are middle terms that are not themselves mediated by other middle terms.

Aristotle asks whether proofs proceed to infinity, whether everything is demonstrable (*An. Pst.* 82a8). Everything is demonstrable if and only if the series of middle terms is dense. However, strictly speaking, with a dense series, there could be no proof of any length. Everything would be demonstrable in the sense that any premiss could be derived from other premisses, but nothing would be demonstrable in the sense that one would never reach principles from which the proof could proceed. Any two terms are separated by middle terms and so that one is predicated of the other can be inferred. In showing that proofs do not proceed to infinity, that not everything is demonstrable, Aristotle shows that the process of filling out a proof will terminate as one encounters, after finitely many steps, non-demonstrable principles.

Aristotle says that the finite length of chains of predication implies that there are non-demonstrable truths from which proof must commence (*An. Pst.* 84a29–b2). Similarly, he argues that the finite length of chains prevents an infinite regress. When constructing a proof, a regress occurs if one continues to use premisses which themselves can be derived. Strictly speaking, it is not the finite character but the non-dense quality of predications that is responsible for these properties of proof. That Aristotle says it is the finite length of chains which prevents a regress provides further evidence that he takes an infinite number of middles between fixed extremes to be dense.

Given this interpretation, an otherwise cryptic remark becomes intelligible:[9]

[9] I am indebted to Kenneth Quandt for showing me that a previous interpretation I had offered of this passage was untenable.

'It makes no difference if someone were to say that some of the $bc \ldots d$ are contiguous so that there are none between them, and that others cannot be taken; for whichever of the c I take, there will be in the direction of b or d infinitely many intermediates or not. It makes no difference from which [term] they are first infinite, whether directly or not, for the [terms] after these are infinite.' (*An. Pst.* 82a30–35)

If there are infinitely many middle terms between the fixed extremes $b \ldots d$, then at least some proper segment $c_i \ldots c_j$ of the middles must be dense. It does not matter if some part of the series, say $bc_0c_1c_2$, is contiguous and some part, say $c_2 \ldots d$, is dense. For no matter which c_i I choose, either there will be infinitely many middle terms separating c_i from b or there will be infinitely many middle terms separating c_i from d. One can thus make sense of the claim:

'It makes no difference from which [term] they are first infinite, whether directly or not, for the [terms] after these are infinite.' (*An. Pst.* 82a33–35)

Initially this claim may appear puzzling. In a series $bc_0c_1c_2 \ldots d$ which immediately after c_2 becomes dense, the infinite series starts not with c_2 but with b. However, since the series is limited by an extreme term d, if it remained contiguous it would be finite. The infinite series starts with c_2 in the sense that it is in virtue of the density of the series, which begins after c_2, that the entire series is infinite.

In *Posterior Analytics* A21, Aristotle uses elegant and simple proof-theoretic techniques to show that if chains of predication are finite – i.e. if the answers to (1) and (2) are negative – then proofs with negative conclusions must be of finite length. He proceeds by cases, examining in every figure a syllogism with a negative conclusion.

Assume a negative answer to (1) and (2). It follows that proofs with a universal affirmative conclusion must be finitely long. For *Barbara* is the only syllogism with a universal affirmative conclusion. So if the premisses are derived, they too must be derived from instances of *Barbara*. But an infinite proof tree in *Barbara*, as already described, is witness to an infinite ordering of a chain of predication between the terms of the conclusion. This is impossible: for a negative answer to (1) and (2) provides a negative answer to (3) – there cannot be an infinite series of middle terms between fixed extremes.

In the first figure a proof of a universal negative conclusion occurs only in *Celarent*:

$$\frac{Ec_0d \quad Abc_0}{Ebd}$$

Either the premisses are principles or they are derived from principles. If Abc_0 is not a principle, the proof of it must be only finitely long. So the proof of Ebd remains finite when the proof of Abc_0 is inserted. If the premiss Ec_0d is not a principle it must arise as the conclusion of a syllogism in either the first or second figure (*Celarent, Cesare, Camestres*). Suppose it arises in *Celarent*, the very form of inference in which it functions as a premiss. Then the premisses must be of the form Ec_1d, Ac_0c_1 and the expanded proof must be:

$$\frac{Ec_1d \quad Ac_0c_1}{\dfrac{Ec_0d \quad Abc_0}{Ebd}}$$

To derive the negative premiss Ec_0d, an appropriate affirmative premiss Ac_0c_1 is required. A chain of affirmative predication is established in which c_0 is predicated of b, and c_1 is in turn predicated of c_0. If the negative premisses are repeatedly derived by the same form of inference, one gets a chain of affirmative predication $bc_0 \ldots c_n c_{n+1} \ldots$ such that each c_{n+1} is predicated of c_n. There will be as many predicates in the chain as there are inference steps in the proof of Ebd. If the proof were infinitely long, with each negative premiss derived in *Celarent*, then there would be an infinite chain of affirmative predication. This is impossible, since a negative answer to (1) is assumed. The other syllogisms with a universal negative conclusion (*Cesare* and *Camestres*) behave in the same way. (The proof is left as an exercise for the interested reader.)

Aristotle is using the syntactic constraints of the syllogistic to investigate what any proof of a universal conclusion must look like. With remarkably modern-looking proof-theoretic techniques he shows that, given the stated assumptions, the proof must be finitely long.

So far it has been assumed that the premisses are derived from a repeated application of a single form of inference. To show that any proof of a universal negative conclusion must be finite, Aristotle must establish that if a proof uses *various* types of inference in deriving premisses, it will nevertheless be finitely long. He offers this argument:

'It is evident that even if it is proved not in one way but in all –
sometimes in the first figure, sometimes in the second or third – that
it will come to a stop even so; for the ways are finite and necessarily
anything finite taken a finite number of times is finite.' (*An. Pst.*
82b29–33)

This argument is not valid. It is true that if one combines a finite
number of extended syllogisms each being of finite length, the resulting
extended syllogism will be finite. However even if one grants that every
extended syllogism which uses repeated application of a single type of
inference can only be finitely long, what reason is there for thinking
that one can only combine a finite number of them? Is it not theoreti-
cally possible to adjoin infinitely many finite syllogisms – each repeatedly
using a single form of inference? In such a case one would have an
infinitely long proof in which any single form of inference would be
used without interruption only a finite number of times.

To provide a valid argument for Aristotle's claim one must answer
two questions. First, are there combinations of inferences that will
break an already established chain of predication? For if every form of
inference solely extends the already existing chain of affirmative predication, then the use of various forms of inference will not disrupt the
chain which forces the proof to be finite. However, if there are inferences that break an already established chain, a second question arises.
Given that chains of predication can be broken in the course of a proof,
will there be at least one chain which, if the proof is carried out far
enough, will continually be resumed and extended? If there is at least
one such chain, then, since it is both finite and continually extended, it
will, regardless of occasional interruption, force the proof to be
finitely long.

The answers to the two questions are, first, that affirmative chains of
predication can be broken in proofs using various inferences but,
second, that in every such proof there is at least one chain that is continually extended throughout the proof. Aristotle is thus correct in his
claim that proofs of negative conclusions using various forms of inference must be finite. Though his argument is invalid, the possibility that
it leaves open – that there might be an infinite number of distinct finite
chains established by a proof – cannot in fact arise.

In a proof using various forms of inference, affirmative chains of
predication can be broken. Suppose one has a proof of a universal negative conclusion *Ebd* which uses various forms of inference. The

immediate inference of the conclusion must be in *Celarent, Cesare* or *Camestres*, as these are the only syllogisms with universal negative conclusions. Suppose the immediate inference of the conclusion is in *Celarent*:

$$\frac{Ec_0d \quad Abc_0}{Ebd}$$

If the negative premiss Ec_0d is itself derived from an instance of *Celarent*, then by arguments given above, after at most a finite number of repeated instances of *Celarent* one reaches a negative premiss, Ec_nd, that is not itself derived from an instance in *Celarent*:

$$Ec_nd$$

.

.

.

$$\frac{Ec_1d \quad Ac_0c_1}{\dfrac{Ec_0d \quad Abc_0}{Ebd}}$$

Through each repeated inference in *Celarent* an affirmative chain of predication has been established – $bc_0c_1 \ldots c_{n-1}c_n$ – in which each member is predicated of its immediate predecessor.

Suppose now that the premiss Ec_nd is not itself a principle but is derived. Then since by assumption it cannot itself be the result of an inference in *Celarent*, it must be the conclusion of an inference in *Cesare* or *Camestres*. The question is whether any form of inference breaks the chain of predication so far established. If the premiss Ec_nd is derived by an instance of *Camestres*, the affirmative chain of predication will be broken. Suppose that Ec_nd and every negative premiss that occurs above it are derived in *Camestres*:

$$\text{Camestres} \quad Adc_{n+1} \quad \frac{Ac_{n+1}c_{n+2} \quad \dfrac{Ac_{n+2}c_{n+3} \quad Ec_nc_{n+3}}{Ec_nc_{n+2}}}{Ec_nc_{n+1}}$$
$$Ec_nd$$

.

.

.

$$\text{Celarent} \quad \frac{Ec_1d \quad Ac_0c_1}{\dfrac{Ec_0d \quad Abc_0}{Ebd}}$$

There are two distinct chains of predication established by this syllogism: $<bc_0 \ldots c_{n-1}c_n>$ and $<dc_{n+1}c_{n+2}c_{n+3}>$. The original chain stops after a finite number of steps and a new chain begins. This chain too can be broken after a finite number of steps while the proof continues.

Since an affirmative chain can be broken, the next question that must be answered is whether throughout a proof of a negative conclusion there will be at least one chain which, though possibly interrupted, will continually be extended throughout the proof. It has been shown that there can be only a finite number of successive repetitions of the same inference in deriving a negative premiss. So one can suppose, without loss of generality, that every premiss is derived by a form of inference different from that in which it serves as premiss. Suppose that the last inference of the proof is in *Celarent*. An examination of the diagram below reveals that no matter how the proof is expanded, there will be at least one chain of predication that continues to be extended.

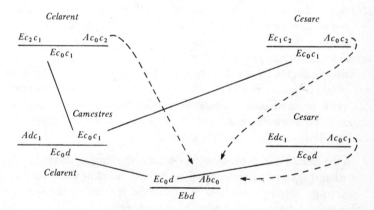

If the first negative premiss in *Celarent* Ec_0d is inferred through *Cesare*, then the affirmative chain of predication $bc_0c_1 \ldots$ is extended without interruption. If the premiss is inferred through *Camestres*, then two affirmative chains – $<bc_0>$ and $<dc_1>$ – are established. But the derivation of the negative premiss in *Camestres*, Ec_0c_1, must serve to extend the original chain of predication: $<bc_0c_2>$. The original chain is interrupted, but as soon as the newly established chain is itself interrupted, the original chain is extended. One cannot form a third distinct chain. A similar result obtains if the immediate inference of the conclusion is *Cesare* or *Camestres*. (Again, the interested reader can verify this himself.)

Therefore, if affirmative chains of predication are finite, proofs with universal negative conclusions must be finite. In fact, even if every successive inference extends a chain distinct from the chain extended by the immediately preceding inference, the entire proof cannot be more than twice as long as one of the chains of predication. The chains of predication established by a proof not only enforce that the proof be finite, but constrain its length to less than or equal to twice the size of one of the chains of predication. (One can easily use this method to show that proofs of particular conclusions, whether negative or affirmative, must be finite.)

The entire argument thus far rests upon the assumption that chains of predication are finite – that the answers to (1) and (2) are negative. *Posterior Analytics* A22 tries to prove this assumption.[10] The strategy is to appeal to a structure implicit in nature. Chains of predication are not abstract mathematical entities; they reflect an order possessed by a subject and its predicates. This order is reflected in the structure of a proof and restricts the proof to finite length. A study of nature can therefore reveal an important property of proofs.

Aristotle begins by considering those predicates which are 'in what something is' (ἐν τῷ τί ἐστι *An. Pst.* 82b37). A primary substance cannot cease to have such a predicate without ceasing to be that substance.[11] To show there are only finitely many such predicates in a subject, Aristotle offers a simple defence:

'In the case of things predicated in what something is, it is clear; for if what it is to be something can be defined or is knowable and one cannot go through infinitely many things, it is necessary that the things predicated in what something is are finite.' (*An. Pst.* 82b37–83a1)

Similarly

'Now either it will be predicated as a substance, i.e. either being the genus or the differentia of what is predicated – but it has been proved

---

10 For a detailed examination of A22 see Hamlyn, 'Aristotle on predication'; Barnes, *Aristotle's Posterior Analytics*, pp. 166–73; Demos, 'The structure of substance according to Aristotle'; Ross, *Aristotle's Prior and Posterior Analytics*, pp. 573–83.

11 Miss Anscombe has suggested the more felicitous translation, 'predicated in the category of substance'. For the sake of uniformity with Barnes' commentary, I will conform to his less felicitous, but literal, translation. For a discussion of such predicates, see Barnes, *Aristotle's Posterior Analytics*, p. 166.

that these will not be infinitely many, either downwards or upwards (e.g. man is two-footed, that is animal, that is something else; nor animal of man, that of Callias, and that of another thing in what something is); for one can define every substance of that kind, but one cannot go through infinitely many things in thought. Hence they are not infinitely many either upwards or downwards; for one cannot define that [substance] of which infinitely many things are predicated.' (*An. Pst.* 83a39–b8)[12]

We are able to define, but we could not think through infinitely many predicates; therefore there are only finitely many predicates in the definition. It is clear that Aristotle believes that these predicates form a chain, '. . . man is two-footed, that is animal, that is something else'.

Aristotle proceeds to consider non-essential predication (*An. Pst.* 83a1–b31). He distinguishes *strict predication* from *incidental predication*. A phrase like 'the white thing is a log' is a degenerate form of predication, for it fails to reveal the metaphysical structure of subject and predicate. It is not that the white thing is the underlying subject which happens to be a log. Rather the log is the underlying subject which happens to be white (*An. Pst.* 83a1–14). Only predications which reveal metaphysical structure are strict and it is with these that proof is concerned (*An. Pst.* 83a15–22).

Predications which are not essential are always predications of an underlying subject. To show that a series of such predications forms a chain, Aristotle rules out the possibility of counterpredication: that c_0 may be predicated of c_1 and c_1 predicated of c_0 (*An. Pst.* 83a36–b10). Aristotle distinguishes predicating from saying truly (*An. Pst.* 83a38). Predication is not merely a linguistic act.[13] Though one can say both 'the white thing is a log' and 'the log is white', only the latter is a genuine predication. One has said both sentences truly, but one has not made a genuine counterpredication.[14] So predications begin with an

---

[12] I translate '*οὐσία*' as 'substance' rather than Barnes' 'reality'. Cf. Barnes, *Aristotle's Posterior Analytics*, p. 169.

[13] See Hamlyn, 'Aristotle on predication', and J. L. Ackrill, *Aristotle's Categories and De Interpretatione*, pp. 71ff.

[14] Ross makes needlessly heavy weather of this passage. He says that the 'connexion with the general argument is particularly hard to seize; any interpretation must be regarded as only conjectural' (Ross, *Aristotle's Prior and Posterior Analytics*, pp. 578–9). Ross admits to being confused that within a proof of the impossibility of infinite proofs '. . . is curiously intermingled a polemic against the possibility of counter-predication. We can connect the two themes, it seems, only by supposing that he is anxious to exclude not one but two kinds of infinite chain; not only a chain leading ever to wider

underlying subject and form a chain. Those predications which are not
essential conform to the categories: '. . . they are either quality or
quantity or relation or doing or undergoing or place or time' (*An. Pst.*
83b16). These qualifications of a subject are finite and so the predications are finite (*An. Pst.* 83b15).

From a modern point of view this argument is not compelling. It is
presented in the context of a metaphysics which is now alien: e.g. we
do not think of predicates as forming chains. Further, in so far as
definition is supposed to reveal what it is to be for a thing (τὸ τί ἦν
εἶναι), there is no reason to believe we are able to give definitions.[15]
That the mind cannot 'go through infinitely many things in thought'
is not obviously true.[16] Aristotle's argument suffers because he is not a
modern: he lived in his world, not ours. For example, he believed that
the basic principles of a science are simply grasped by mental insight
(νοῦς) (*An. Pst.* B19). The modern problem that we may never know
the basic principles of a science, that the human mind may be funda-
mentally incapable of understanding the structure of the universe, does

---

[15] See Kripke, 'Naming and necessity'.

[16] Given Aristotle's conception of the infinite, to say that the process of defining terminates is equivalent to saying that it terminates after finitely many steps. It does seem
as though one cannot have an infinite number of distinct thoughts; each thought being
that a distinct predicate is true of a single subject. This is because each thought is
assumed to take a discrete and uniform length of time, and we only live through
finitely many such lengths. Nevertheless there is a similar claim – that a single predicate
can be seen to hold of an infinite number of subjects – that does not seem so implausible.
Consider, for example, an omega-rule of inference: $\dfrac{F(0),\ F(1),\ F(2)\cdots}{(x)F(x)}$. By Gödel's
theorem there are formulas of elementary number theory such that for any n one can
prove $F(n)$ a theorem, but for which one cannot prove, within a particular consistent
system, $(x)F(x)$. Adjoining to the original system an omega-rule, one can make the
needed inference. If one forms a new system by adjoining an omega-rule one can prove (x)
$F(x)$ and thus that the original system is consistent. Gentzen–Schütte type consistency
proofs are generally thought to prove elementary number theory consistent. But one is
not justified in detaching the conclusion $(x)F(x)$ which is exactly what one does if one
takes consistency to be proved, unless one has established that $F(0)$, $F(1)$ ... Of
course we do not have to have infinitely many distinct thoughts – that $F(n)$ for each
n – each taking a discrete and uniform amount of time. We can see that $F(\ )$ is true of
each n in virtue of the proof that $F(\ )$ holds of any particular number.

---

predicates, but also one which is infinite in the sense that it returns upon itself, as a ring
does (*Phys.* 207a2).' Ironically the passage Ross cites, *Physics* 207a2ff, provides direct
evidence against his interpretation. For there Aristotle rejects circular movement, in
itself, as a truly infinitary concept. Aristotle is not, *pace* Ross, trying to reject some
deviant type of infinitary chain. Rather he is simply trying to show that predication in
fact forms a chain. The passage stands, on the Ross interpretation, as a curious inter-
mezzo in an otherwise concise and brilliantly argued proof.

not arise. Yet though the foundation of Aristotle's argument must strike us as unconvincing, on the basis of it he is able to offer a truly remarkable compactness proof, containing the seeds of proof-theoretic techniques which would not be employed again until this century.

3

Hypothetical syllogisms

At the beginning of *Prior Analytics* A23, Aristotle says he will show how all syllogisms without qualification are formed through the syllogistic figures (*An. Pr.* 40b20–22). In this passage Aristotle is harking back to his wide-ranging definition of syllogism as a *logos* in which, certain things being posited, something other than what is posited follows of necessity from their being so (*An. Pr.* 24b18–20). The point of A23 is to investigate to what extent the syllogistic is adequate for the formalization of deductive arguments.

Aristotle divides all syllogisms into those which are *direct* and those which are *hypothetical*, one example of the latter being syllogism *per impossibile*[1] (*An. Pr.* 40b22–26). He discusses direct syllogisms first, he says, because it is in virtue of this discussion that it will become clear how hypothetical syllogisms in general, and syllogisms *per impossibile* in particular, are brought about through the syllogistic figures (*An. Pr.* 40b26–29). As discussed in Chapter 1, Aristotle presents an abstract argument designed to show that direct syllogisms can be formalized in the syllogistic. Hypothetical syllogisms are thought to be formalizable in the syllogistic *only* in so far as each contains, as a proper part, a direct syllogism (*An. Pr.* 41a37–41b1). In a hypothetical syllogism that is not of the *per impossibile* variety, one attempts to persuade someone of a conclusion Q by getting him to agree to accept Q if P is proved. One then proves P directly. The form of the argument is thus:

(H) 'You agree to accept Q, if P; but ... so P; but you agreed to accept Q, if P; therefore you must accept Q.'

The part of the argument '..., so P' is a direct syllogism and is thus assumed to be syllogistically formalizable (cf. also *An. Pr.* A44 50a16–28). Similarly with *per impossibile* syllogisms: *only* because each contains a direct syllogism is any part of a *per impossibile* syllogism thought to be formalizable in the syllogistic (*An. Pr.* 41a32–37). In a *per*

---

[1] The phrase 'ἐξ ὑποθέσεως' is a term of art for Aristotle. I have translated it uniformly as 'hypothetical' or 'hypothetically' rather than write the Greek or a transliteration. An alternative translation is 'from a hypothesis'. Whichever translation (or lack of it) one prefers, one must keep in mind that Aristotle is using the phrase in a precise and technical sense.

impossibile syllogism Aristotle says one directly deduces a falsehood and then proves the conclusion hypothetically when something impossible results from supposing the contradictory of that which one wishes to prove (*An. Pr.* 41a23–26). Therefore, one form a *per impossibile* syllogism may take is:

(PI$_1$) P, suppose *not-Q*, then R; but that is impossible; therefore Q.

The first part of the *per impossibile* syllogism

P, suppose *not-Q*, then R

is a direct syllogism, and, by Aristotle's earlier argument, can thus be expressed in syllogistic form. Aristotle does not think that the entire *per impossibile* syllogism can be formalized as a chain of syllogistic inferences.

Why does Aristotle, in a chapter devoted to showing the adequacy of the syllogistic for formalizing deductive arguments, discuss hypothetical syllogisms at all? It is not as though Aristotle fallaciously believed the entire hypothetical syllogism could be formalized. If he had one could imagine hypothetical syllogisms being treated as a tier in an architectonic designed to show that all syllogisms were syllogistically formalizable. But Aristotle is well aware that hypothetical syllogisms present a problem for the syllogistic. When he concludes *Prior Analytics* A23 by saying that the arguments of the chapter have shown that all proof and all syllogism necessarily *come about through* the three syllogistic figures, he is actually making a remarkably weak claim. He has not claimed to show that every syllogism in the broad sense is formalizable. He has only claimed to show that every direct syllogism is formalizable and that the hypothetical syllogism contains a direct syllogism as a proper part. Why admit an acknowledged recalcitrant example?

Commentators have interpreted Aristotle as concerned with giving an analysis of deductions with a conditional premiss, 'If P, then Q', within the confines of the syllogistic.[2] On this interpretation, Aristotle wishes to describe deductions from a conditional, but is faced with the fact that the syllogistic is inadequate both for the formalization of conditional statements and of inferences from them. This picture does not

[2] Cf. W. and M. Kneale, *The Development of Logic*, pp. 98ff; Mueller, 'Greek mathematics and Greek logic'; Patzig, *Aristotle's Theory of the Syllogism*, p. 149; Łukasiewicz, *Aristotle's Syllogistic From the Standpoint of Modern Formal Logic*, p. 49.

go to the heart of the matter. It cannot provide a unified account of hypothetical syllogisms, because it does not acknowledge that the underlying problem is not with the *formalization* of certain statements, or inferences, but with the *role* certain statements play within an argument.

There is an important feature of deductive arguments which the definition of a formal deduction tends to ignore: that is the argumentative role of each sentence in the deduction.[3] A formal deduction is often defined as a sequence of sentences, the last member being the conclusion, such that every member is either an axiom or a premiss or the conclusion of a rule of inference from previous members.[4] But this disjunctive property is too weak to yield an actual deductive argument from premisses to conclusion. One does not know which sentences are inferred by which rules from which previously occurring sentences. Neither does one know which sentences – the axioms and consequences of axioms – are being asserted and which are merely entertained; so one does not know whether the formal deduction represents an unconditional proof of the conclusion or only a deduction from certain supposed premisses. A formal deduction, so defined, provides at most a guarantee that a deductive argument from premisses to conclusion exists.

Frege insisted that one must distinguish between the thought expressed by a sentence and the assertion of its truth.[5] A sentence may occur in discourse both asserted and unasserted, yet the content of the sentence remains constant. For example, the sentence may be uttered as part of a more complex sentence, such as in the antecedent of a conditional in which the whole sentence is being asserted, not simply the antecedent. If one is to recognize e.g. *modus ponens* – From P and *If P then Q*, infer Q – as a valid inference one must recognize the same thought P as occurring in one context where it is asserted and in another where it is not. Further, one can utter a sentence within the context of some convention that the sentence is understood not to be asserted: if, for example, one is asked to imagine or suppose that certain sentences are true.

Why has so little attention been paid, before and after Frege, to the role of assertion in deductive argumentation? One reason, suggested by

---

[3] See Shoesmith and Smiley, *Multiple Conclusion Logic*, p. 106.
[4] Cf. e.g. Mendelson, *Introduction to Mathematical Logic*, p. 30.
[5] See Frege, 'Thoughts', *Logical Investigations*, pp. 1–30; Geach, *Logic Matters*, pp. 250–69.

Geach and Dummett, is that our use of language presupposes that the utterances of indicative sentences are assertions unless some special convention is introduced whereby we recognize that the sentences are not being asserted.[6] It is assumed that in communication people tell us what they take to be true – or even when lying they tell us what they want us to interpret them as taking to be true – so in spoken or printed discourse one need not introduce some convention indicating that one is asserting what one says. Rather one must make it clear when one wishes to *withdraw* assertoric force from one's utterances. Thus since discourse takes place against a background of presumed assertion one would expect attention to be paid not to the pervasive phenomenon of assertion, but to the singular cases where the phenomenon is absent. Further, within the realm of deductive arguments one is forced to pay attention to the absence of assertive force even more rarely than in ordinary discourse. Of course, not all deductions are proofs, but even in the course of a direct deduction of a conclusion Q from a set of premisses X, it does not matter for the deduction itself whether or not the premisses are actually being asserted. Only after the deduction is completed do we need to consider whether we have actually proved Q or simply deduced Q from X. For example, in an Aristotelian context, we can form a syllogism and then check whether the ultimate premisses are first principles of a science, commonly held beliefs, or, indeed, known falsehoods. In the latter cases we only have a deduction from premisses to conclusion and not a proof, but that need not have affected the formation of the syllogism. It is only in those cases in which one needs to recognize the *lack* of assertive force in order to describe the deduction itself – such as when suppositions are introduced only to be discharged at a later stage in the deduction – that one must pay attention to the force of the sentences in the deduction.

Natural deduction systems, developed by Gentzen and Jaśkowski, provide a formalism which easily accommodates the introduction and discharge of suppositions.[7] Gentzen observed that a formal system which permits the entertainment and discharge of suppositions can present formal derivations more in accord with non-formal mathematical proof and argument than formal systems which do not. His natural deduction system allows one to distinguish the argumentative roles of

---

[6] See Geach, *Logic Matters*, p. 262; Dummett, *Frege: Philosophy of Language*, p. 302.

[7] Gentzen, 'Investigations into logical deduction'; Jaśkowski, 'On the rules of suppositions in formal logic'. To see how easy it is to annotate a deduction in a natural deduction system, see Fitch, *Symbolic Logic, An Introduction; Elements of Combinatory Logic*; Lemmon, *Beginning Logic*.

sentences occurring in a deduction. One can distinguish between premisses, upon which the proof of the conclusion depends, and suppositions which are introduced in the course of the deduction, and their consequences pursued, but on which the conclusion does not depend. For example, let

$$
\begin{array}{ll}
X & \text{premisses} \\
\neg Q & \text{supposition} \\
\cdot & \\
\cdot & \\
\cdot & \\
R &
\end{array}
$$

be a deduction of R from the set of premisses X and the supposition $\neg Q$. Then it is common in natural deduction systems to have some form of *rule of reductio ad absurdum*:[8]

$$
\begin{array}{lll}
X & Y & \text{premisses} \\
\neg Q & \neg Q & \text{supposition} \\
\cdot & \cdot & \\
\cdot & \cdot & \\
\cdot & \cdot & \\
R & \neg R & \\
\hline
& Q &
\end{array}
$$

The conclusion Q does depend on the premisses X and Y but not on the supposition $\neg Q$. Natural deduction systems enable us to take some account of argumentative force by distinguishing premisses from suppositions, but we need not think of all premisses as being asserted:[9] we may only be constructing a deduction of a conclusion from premisses we do not believe. However, with suppositions we must explicitly recognize that they are *not* being asserted, but only supposed. The premisses may or may not be asserted; from the standpoint of describing the deduction we may treat them all as though they were being asserted. With suppositions, by contrast, one must acknowledge that they are being supposed in order to describe their temporary entertainment in the course of a deduction.

Gentzen criticized the formal systems of Frege, Russell and Hilbert, which do not contain any mechanism for recognizing suppositions. Deductions in those systems tend to be cumbrous and do not reflect the character of non-formal deductions. With a natural deduction system one can provide an accurate picture of a deduction in which it is

---

[8] Cf. e.g. Lemmon, *Beginning Logic*, p. 40.
[9] Cf. Dummett, *Frege: Philosophy of Language*, p. 309.

essential that certain sentences are recognized as being supposed and not asserted.

Aristotle's syllogistic, like the formal systems of Frege, Russell and Hilbert, makes no provision for the explicit recognition of suppositions. This insight is essential if one is to make sense of Aristotle's remarks on hypothetical syllogisms. His treatment of these syllogisms reflects his, perhaps belated, awareness that there are certain types of argument which cannot be analysed without recourse to the notion of argument-ative role. The syllogistic does not allow for an expression of argu-mentative role, and it is precisely with hypothetical syllogisms that Aristotle faces this inadequacy.

Why should Aristotle have countenanced hypothetical syllogisms at all? One reason may be that in trying to show that all syllogisms can to some extent be formalized, Aristotle wished to cast the net so widely that it included rigorous dialectical arguments as well as mathematical deductions. Since the goal is only to show that non-direct deductions are partially formalizable, Aristotle is at liberty to construe what he takes to be a syllogism quite loosely. Hypothetical syllogisms represent Aristotle's analysis of the type of debate that occurred in the Academy. Shorey has argued that to understand hypothetical syllogisms one must examine the form of Platonic debate.[10] In the Dialogues, Platonic argu-ments take the form of debate or common inquiry. For either debate or inquiry to proceed some degree of agreement between speakers is necessary. The principles of dialectic are statements to which all parties are willing to agree. Unlike Aristotelian methodology which recognizes particular principles specific to each science, in Platonic debate the speakers move back until they reach some principle to which they can all agree. In Aristotle's hypothetical syllogism, the agreement would be to accept Q, if it can be shown that P.

But the major reason that Aristotle discusses hypothetical syllogisms in *Prior Analytics* A23 must be that he considered the *per impossibile* syllogism to be a type of hypothetical syllogism. Proof by means of a *per impossibile* technique was a method with which Aristotle was evi-dently familiar: he regularly cites as an example the proof of the incommensurability of the diagonal of a square with its sides (cf. e.g. *An. Pr.* 41a26, 50a37). In a discussion of the adequacy of the syllogistic for formalizing deductions, it would have been difficult for Aristotle to have ignored the *per impossibile* syllogism. There is textual evidence for

10 Paul Shorey, '*Συλλογισμοὶ ἐξ ὑποθέσεως* in Aristotle'.

this conjecture. Immediately upon completing the argument for the formalizability of direct syllogisms, Aristotle begins an extended discussion not of hypothetical syllogisms in general, but of the special case of *per impossibile* syllogisms (*An. Pr.* 41a20–37). It is only these arguments for which there is need to show that they can, to some extent, be formalized. All other hypothetical syllogisms, by contrast, receive only the most cursory mention in *Prior Analytics* A23 (41a37–b1). It is maintained only that a similar argument to that which has been worked out for *per impossibile* syllogisms will apply to hypothetical syllogisms generally. The *per impossibile* syllogism and the other types of hypothetical syllogism each contain a direct syllogism as a proper part.

However, why should Aristotle consider the *per impossibile* syllogism to be a *type* of hypothetical syllogism? The claim is not merely that the two syllogisms share the structural similarity of containing a direct syllogism. It is, rather, that a *per impossibile* syllogism is an instance of a hypothetical syllogism. The reason, I conjecture, is that Aristotle assimilates the role of *supposition* in *per impossibile* syllogisms to the role of *agreement* in other types of hypothetical syllogisms. What is important about each syllogism is that one must explicitly recognize that a certain step has a special argumentative role; and Aristotle was not careful to distinguish among types of roles. Consider the beginning of *Prior Analytics* A44:

'Further we must not try to reduce hypothetical syllogisms; for with the given premisses it is not possible to reduce them. For they have not been proved by syllogism, but all are *assented* to by *agreement*. For instance if a man should *suppose* that unless there is one faculty of contraries, there cannot be one science and should then argue that not every faculty is of contraries, e.g. of what is healthy and what is sickly: for the same thing will then be at the same time healthy and sickly. He has shown that there is not one faculty of all contraries, but he has not proved that there is not a science. And yet one must *agree*. But the *agreement* does not come from a syllogism but from an hypothesis. This cannot be reduced: but the argument that there is not a single faculty can. The argument perhaps was a syllogism: but the other was an hypothesis.' (*An. Pr.* A44, 50a16–28; my emphasis)[11]

---

[11] 'Faculty' translates 'δύναμις': another acceptable translation in this context might be 'potentiality'.

Here supposition is clearly being assimilated to agreement. We are being presented with an instance of a hypothetical syllogism which, as we have seen, has the form:

(H) You agree to accept Q, if P; but . . . ., so P; but you agreed to accept Q, if P; therefore you must accept Q.

In this example, the agreement should be to accept that there cannot be one science, if it can be shown that there is not one faculty of contraries. Yet it is precisely this step which Aristotle says is being supposed. One reason for this assimilation may be that hypothetical syllogisms represent Aristotle's analysis of rigorous debate as it occurred in the Academy. In such debate one need not secure an undying commitment from one's interlocutor to accept Q, if P is proved. All that is required is that he agree, *for the sake of the argument*, to accept Q if P is proved. Of course, not any P will do: it must be a P such that the interlocutor has some reason to think that its truth will ensure the truth of Q. Otherwise he will not agree, even for the sake of argument. So even in this case the interlocutor is being asked to do more than suppose that if P, then Q. Nevertheless, agreement for the sake of argument and supposition do seem to be related, if only as distant cousins. The important feature which hypothetical and *per impossibile* syllogisms share – and which may mask the differences between agreement and supposition – is that one must adopt a specific attitude toward one of the steps of the argument.[12] Supposition is a feature which the syllogistic does not easily accommodate. Thus it should come as no surprise that, in the quoted passage, Aristotle cautions against trying to reduce hypothetical syllogisms to the perfect syllogisms of the first figure (*An. Pr.* 50a16; 50a26). For only a proper part – the direct syllogism – can be rendered in syllogistic form and it is only for this part that one has any ground for believing reduction possible.

An air of paradox surrounds the quoted passage. Aristotle both calls hypothetical syllogisms 'syllogisms' and says of them that the conclusion is *not* reached by syllogism, but hypothetically (*An. Pr.* 50a25–28). One can make sense of this apparent contradiction. Aristotle has reason to treat a hypothetical syllogism as a syllogism. A syllogism is a *logos* in which certain things being posited (τίθημι) something else follows of necessity from their being so (*An. Pr.*

---

[12] From now on I will use 'supposition' in a broad sense to cover both supposition as it occurs in a *per impossibile* syllogism and agreement for the sake of argument as it occurs in a hypothetical syllogism.

24b18–20). The verb '$\tau i \theta \eta \mu \iota$' (to posit, lay down) is usually neutral with respect to the argumentative force with which premisses are employed,[13] and, on occasion, is specifically used to describe a statement that must clearly be supposed and not asserted in the course of the argument. For example, Aristotle says that in *per impossibile* syllogisms one proves the conclusion hypothetically when something impossible results from the *supposition* ($\tau i \theta \eta \mu \iota$) of the contradictory (*An. Pr.* 41a25–26). Similarly in the proof of the incommensurability of the diagonal, the absurd result that an odd number is equal to an even comes about through *supposing* ($\tau i \theta \eta \mu \iota$) that the diagonal is commensurate (*An. Pr.* 41a27, 50a37). The contradictory of the conclusion is clearly supposed and not asserted in a *per impossibile* syllogism so that, in these passages at least, one must not take the verb $\tau i \theta \eta \mu \iota$ to imply any assertive force. Thus a hypothetical syllogism does qualify as a syllogism. The premiss 'Q, if P' and those premisses needed to deduce P are posited ($\tau i \theta \eta \mu \iota$) and Q follows of necessity from their being so.

Yet Aristotle also says that the conclusion of a hypothetical syllogism is not reached by syllogism but hypothetically (*An. Pr.* 50a23–28). This remark must cause problems for anyone who wishes to treat a hypothetical syllogism merely as a deduction from a conditional premiss. For if the conditional is functioning like any other premiss, why does not Aristotle simply recognize that one has a valid syllogism that contains a conditional premiss? If, however, one takes Aristotle's central concern to be with argumentative role, then two explanations emerge as to why he says the conclusion is reached not by syllogism but hypothetically. First, in hypothetical argument one is meant to be arguing *unconditionally* to a conclusion Q. One is not simply deducing Q from a set of premisses that include 'If P, then Q'. One is attempting to persuade one's interlocutor to admit Q. To this end one secures his agreement to accept Q if P is proved: but this strategy is designed to force him to assent to Q. If the argument was only meant to establish Q conditionally, then one could choose any antecedent R for which one happened to have a proof and trivially prove Q (hypothetically) from the conditional 'If R, then Q'. But one cannot do this in a hypothetical syllogism. One must find a P on the basis of which one's interlocutor is willing to assent to Q. The point of a hypothetical argument is to get one's interlocutor to accept Q, not merely the conditional 'If P, then Q'; thus one must not only carefully secure the interlocutor's agree-

---

[13] See Smiley, 'What is a syllogism?', p. 138.

ment to make certain transitions, one must recognize that the conclusion is not established merely by syllogism, but also on the basis of the antecedent agreement. If, as conjectured, Aristotle discussed hypothetical syllogisms in *Prior Analytics* A23 because he wished to see to what extent rigorous dialectical arguments could be formalized, one would also expect him to discuss to what extent such 'syllogisms' fail to be syllogisms.

Second, Aristotle would, I think, find something discomfiting about the notion of a deduction of a conclusion from an *unasserted* premiss, where that premiss happens to be a conditional. For one naively thinks of a deduction as some sort of step-by-step process in which one comes to see that the conclusion is a logical consequence of the premisses. A fundamental assumption of Aristotle's theory of perfection is that one must be able to be brought to see that a logical consequence holds. The existence of an unasserted conditional in the premisses, however, is designed to compensate for our very inability to reveal the conclusion as a logical consequence of the asserted premisses. By supposing the conditional one supposes that a consequence relation exists in the exact place where one cannot show it to exist. It is as though one assumes a deduction exists to bridge the gap that one cannot close by actually providing a deduction. Thus it is misleading to say one has a deduction of a conclusion Q from a set of premisses X where X contains the premisses needed to prove P and a supposed but unasserted conditional 'If P, then Q'. For one has no idea how much logical space must be travelled – if indeed it is possible at all – to show that if P is true then Q will be true. A more accurate picture of what has been deduced would place the conditional as the antecedent of a conditional conclusion: 'If *If P, then Q*; then Q'. One has deduced this from the premisses needed to prove P.

If one interprets hypothetical syllogisms primarily as Aristotle's attempt to formalize deductions with a conditional premiss it remains a mystery why Aristotle did not simply allow that the conditional could be asserted, recognize *modus ponens* as a rule of inference and accept such arguments as proper syllogisms.[14] If, however, one interprets Aristotle as primarily concerned with argumentative role this mystery does not arise. A familiar form of argument in Aristotle's time happened to begin by securing a conditional agreement from one's interlocutor. Aristotle is not concerned with conditional premisses *per se*; he is concerned with the most common example of argument with an explicitly

14 Cf. Mueller, 'Greek mathematics and Greek logic', p. 55.

supposed premiss – as opposed to one with premisses which could be supposed or asserted indifferently.

Evidence for this interpretation is provided by Aristotle's discussion of what it is to know hypothetically. Hypothetical knowledge is contrasted unfavourably with unqualified knowledge. If one could not know the ultimate premisses of a proof, then one would not know the conclusion unconditionally, but only hypothetically (*An. Pst.* A3, 72b14; cf. 83b39, 84a6). Here what is known hypothetically need not be a conditional. Aristotle did think that the principles of a demonstrative science could be known. This may partially explain why he described hypothetical syllogisms in terms of dialectical debate: in demonstrative science hypothetical syllogisms need never occur.

If one takes hypothetical syllogisms to be deductions from a conditional premiss, it is also difficult to see why *per impossibile* syllogisms should be classified as hypothetical. The Kneales, who take Aristotle to be discussing arguments with conditional premisses, think Aristotle ought to be describing the logical distinction between *modus ponendo ponens* $\dfrac{\text{If } P, \text{ then } Q; P}{Q}$ and *modus tollendo tollens* $\dfrac{\text{If } P \text{ then } Q; \neg Q.}{\neg P}$[15]

But, as the Kneales note with consternation, Aristotle does not make the logical distinction between arguments which affirm the antecedent and those which deny the consequent of a conditional. Rather Aristotle makes what for the Kneales must be the cryptic epistemological point that in *per impossibile* syllogisms, as opposed to other hypothetical syllogisms, there is no need for prior agreement because 'the falsity is obvious' (*An. Pr.* 50a36). Patzig, who also believes there must be a conditional premiss hidden in the works, interprets this statement as claiming that *per impossibile* syllogisms depend on a suppressed, rather than explicit, conditional premiss, 'If not *not-Q*, then *Q*'.[16] Yet there is no textual evidence that Aristotle thought the validity of a *per impossibile* syllogism depended on a, perhaps suppressed, conditional premiss. If a *reductio* strategy is valid at all, then it is valid as Aristotle describes it (*An. Pr.* 40b20–37), without a conditional premiss.

If one interprets a hypothetical syllogism as one which demands explicit acknowledgement of a suppositional step, then *per impossibile* syllogisms are clearly hypothetical. *Per impossibile* syllogisms differ from direct deductions in that in the former one cannot even give a

---

[15] W. & M. Kneale, *The Development of Logic*, pp. 98ff.
[16] Patzig, *Aristotle's Theory of the Syllogism*, p. 149.

formal description without paying some attention to the argumentative role of the sentence occurring in the argument. As mentioned above, one can give a formal analysis of a direct deduction which is neutral with respect to whether the sentences in it are being asserted, supposed, entertained etc. However, even in a purely formal analysis of a deduction by *reductio ad absurdum* some clue must be given as to which statement the derivation of a contradiction is intended to overthrow. A rule of *reductio ad absurdum* may not pay obvious attention to supposition. For example, it may state

$$\begin{array}{cc} \neg P & \neg P \\ \cdot & \cdot \\ \cdot & \cdot \\ \cdot & \cdot \\ Q & \neg Q \\ \hline & P \end{array}$$

but by segregating $\neg P$ from other premisses which may occur in the deductions of Q and of $\neg Q$, the rule has tacitly isolated the sentence which is being temporarily supposed. (Of course, if $\neg P$ is the only premiss that occurs in the deductions of Q and of $\neg Q$, then no segregation is needed. But *reductio* rules are not generally restricted to such cases.) Every syllogistic inference is from two premisses. Hence Aristotle must note, in his analysis of a *per impossibile* syllogism, which premiss is being supposed so as to make clear what the derivation of a falsehood should lead one to reject. To analyse *reductio* arguments one must note that at some stage a supposition is made.

This interpretation would suggest that the *hypothesis* in a *per impossibile* syllogism is the premiss that is being supposed in the direct deduction of a falsehood. That is, the hypothesis is the contradictory of the desired conclusion of the *per impossibile* syllogism. However, there are two strands of textual evidence which seem to impugn this suggestion and thus cast doubt on the interpretation as a whole:

(1) Aristotle often says that in a *per impossibile* syllogism one first directly deduces a falsehood and then infers the ultimate conclusion hypothetically (*An. Pr.* 41a24–25, 41a29, 41a34, 50a32). The structure, as Aristotle is aware (*An. Pr.* 41a37ff), is similar to other hypothetical syllogisms in which one first directly deduces a conclusion P and then moves *hypothetically* to a conclusion Q. In order to make sense of this similar structure commentators have wanted to find a conditional in the

per impossibile syllogism which licenses the transition from the derivation of a falsehood to the inference of the contradictory of the supposed
premiss.[17] They point (*a*) to the awkwardness of taking the 'hypothesis' in a *per impossibile* syllogism to be the contradictory of the conclusion since this does not alone permit the transition Aristotle labels
'hypothetical', and (*b*) to the structural dissimilarities between *per
impossibile* and other *hypothetical* syllogisms that would result from
taking the contradictory of the conclusion as the hypothesis.

(2) Aristotle is often interpreted as saying that *per impossibile* syllogisms differ from other hypothetical syllogisms in that one need not
previously agree to the hypothesis before carrying out the direct
deduction because the falsity of the derived conclusion is obvious[18] (cf.
50a32–38). Thus the hypothesis could not be the explicitly supposed
premiss of the *per impossibile* syllogism. It is conjectured either that the
hypothesis might be a suppressed axiom in the form of a conditional[19]
or that the hypothesis is the contradictory of the derived conclusion,
which need not be explicitly stated since the conclusion is so obviously
false.[20]

Yet nothing Aristotle says need be construed as evidence that the
supposed premiss in a *per impossibile* syllogism is not the hypothesis. In
response to (1): Dummett has noted that supposition differs from
assertion in that it is possible only as a preparation for further linguistic
acts.[21] One cannot simply make a supposition and then stop. There must
be some point to having made the supposition. Let us call this the
linguistic obligation of a supposition. For both hypothetical and *per
impossibile* syllogisms it is quite clear how this obligation is fulfilled.
Having agreed to accept *Q*, if *P*, and confronted with a proof of *P*, one
fulfils one's linguistic obligation by accepting *Q*. Had one not done so

---

[17] Cf. Ross, *Aristotle's Prior and Posterior Analytics*, p. 372: 'But another element in the
hypothesis is brought out in *An. Pst.* 77a22–5 where A. says that *reductio* assumes the
law of excluded middle; i.e. it assumes that if the contradictory of the proposition to be
proved is shown to be false, that proposition must be true.' Mueller, 'Greek mathematics and Greek logic', p. 56: 'One might then consider the hypothesis of a *reductio*
to be the law of propositional logic "(P → (Q & — Q) → — P)" ...' Patzig, *Aristotle's
Theory of the Syllogism*, p. 149: 'The "hypothesis" on which the *per impossibile* procedure rests is that A be regarded as proved if Not (not-A) is proved.'

[18] Cf. Ross, *Aristotle's Prior and Posterior Analytics*, Patzig, *Aristotle's Theory of the
Syllogism*, Mueller, 'Greek mathematics and Greek logic'.

[19] Patzig, *Aristotle's Theory of the Syllogism*, Mueller, 'Greek mathematics and Greek
logic'.

[20] Ross, *Aristotle's Prior and Posterior Analytics*, p. 417.

[21] Dummett, *Frege: Philosophy of Language*, p. 313.

there would have been no point in making the original agreement.[22]
Similarly in a *per impossibile* syllogism: having deduced a contradiction
from the supposition, one then fulfils one's linguistic obligation by
inferring its contradictory.[23] It is precisely this fulfilment of the linguistic obligation that, for Aristotle, is the inference 'from a hypothesis'.
Only if one assumes that the hypothesis must always explicitly license
the transition from a directly deduced conclusion to the conclusion
inferred hypothetically, need one be tempted to think that the supposition of a *per impossibile* syllogism could not be the hypothesis. There is
no evidence to warrant this assumption. If, by contrast, one assumes
that the hypothetical inference is that which fulfils the linguistic obligation incurred by making a supposition, then not only is it most natural
to take the supposition of a *per impossibile* to be the hypothesis, but
analogy between *per impossibile* and other hypothetical syllogisms is
preserved. Though Aristotle generally pays little attention to the
details of formalization he does notice that the fulfilment of obligation –
a hallmark of informal argument – cannot be formalized (*An. Pr.* A44).
This is the part of the argument he calls hypothetical. It is the fulfilment
of the linguistic obligation incurred by the original supposition, and it
is totally irrelevant whether or not the supposition is a conditional.

In response to (2): Aristotle says that *per impossibile* syllogisms differ
from other hypothetical syllogisms in that the latter require a preliminary agreement, whereas in *per impossibile* syllogisms there is no preliminary agreement 'because the falsity is evident' (*An. Pr.* 50a32–37).
It is easy to misinterpret Aristotle.[24] First, since the preliminary
agreement in the hypothetical syllogism is to the hypothesis 'If *P*,
then *Q*', one may be led to believe that the absence of a preliminary
agreement in the *per impossibile* syllogism means that no hypothesis
explicitly occurs at the beginning of a *per impossibile* syllogism. All
Aristotle says however is that there is no preliminary agreement. It is
not that one does not have to agree to a hypothesis: one does not have

---

[22] Do not confuse the fulfilment of a linguistic obligation with the discharge of a supposition in a natural deduction system. The fulfilment of obligation occurs when, having
agreed to accept *Q* if *P* is proved, and confronted with a proof of *P*, one accepts *Q*. This
bears no relation to the situation in a natural deduction where one supposes *P*, deduces
Q, and then discharges the supposition by inferring *If P then Q*.

[23] Here the fulfilment of linguistic obligation and the discharge of a supposition as it
occurs in natural deduction coincide.

[24] This is partly due to the fact that the translations of the relevant passages are misleading.
The translators have tended to read their interpretation into the text. The reader who
wishes to check the various interpretations, including my own, is strongly advised to
use the Greek text and not rely on any translation.

to agree to anything at all. Aristotle does not say that no hypothesis occurs at the beginning of the *per impossibile* syllogism. Indeed a hypothesis does occur at the beginning of the *per impossibile* syllogism, but it is not a preliminary agreement; it is a supposition entertained *during the course* of the syllogism. Second, Ross interprets Aristotle as saying that while in a hypothetical syllogism one must explicitly agree to a hypothesis 'If P, then Q' because it is not obvious, in a *per impossibile* syllogism –

(PI$_2$) P, suppose *not-Q*, then R; therefore Q

– one need not explicitly state the 'hypothesis' *not-R*, since R is obviously false.[25] For example, having deduced from the supposition that the diagonal is commensurate with its side that a given integer is both odd and even, one immediately infers that the diagonal is incommensurate (*An. Pr.* 50a37–38). One need not interpose the 'hypothesis' that no number is both odd and even. Ross has, in fact, isolated the reason why Aristotle only demands that one derive a *falsehood* rather than a *contradiction* in a *per impossibile* syllogism (cf. e.g. *An. Pr.* 41a24). Since the derived conclusion is *obviously* false, there is no need to derive its contradictory. There is, however, no reason to treat the contradictory of the directly derived conclusion as the hypothesis of a *per impossibile* syllogism. All that Aristotle says is that in *per impossibile* syllogisms, unlike other hypothetical syllogisms, one need not enter into an explicit preliminary agreement. It does not follow that there must be something else which is left implicit. Aristotle would have recognized arguments of the form

(PI$_3$) P, suppose *not-Q*, then R, but *not-R*; therefore Q

to be *per impossibile* syllogisms. Even if the step '. . . but *not-R*' does not occur in the proof, there is no reason why it should be treated as the hypothesis of the argument.

The point of Aristotle's distinction is not difficult to discern if one is not committed to finding a hidden hypothesis. Aristotle notes that it is a feature of *per impossibile* syllogisms that one does not merely deduce a falsehood, but an obvious falsehood (cf. e.g. *An. Pr.* 50a36). If one deduced a falsehood not recognized to be such, one would not be in a position to infer the contradictory of the supposition. Precisely because one deduces an *obvious* falsehood R, Aristotle does not insist that one deduce the contradiction R and *not-R* before inferring Q. Were R not

[25] Ross, *Aristotle's Prior and Posterior Analytics*, p. 417.

obviously false, one would have to derive a contradiction. (This might in turn lead to a 'preliminary agreement' to the premiss *not-R*, but it is hard to understand why anyone who could not recognize *R* as false would be willing to accept *not-R* as a premiss.)

There is no textual evidence that stands in the way of interpreting the supposition of a *per impossibile* syllogism as the hypothesis. And there *is* textual evidence in favour of the identification. Aristotle repeatedly refers to the supposed premiss in a *per impossibile* syllogism as the hypothesis. (Cf. e.g. *An. Pr.* 62a4, 61b36, 63a9, 63a15, 63a26, 63a30, 63a33, 63a36, 63a41, 63b4, 63b6, 63b9. Also, cf. 41a30–32.)

To understand Aristotle's attitude toward *per impossibile* syllogisms, it is important to grasp the significance of what he calls the *conversion* of a syllogism. In conversion one takes either the contrary or the contradictory of the conclusion of a syllogism and in conjunction with one of the premisses one deduces the contrary or the contradictory of the other premiss (*An. Pr.* B8, 59b1–6). Only the conversion involving the taking of contradictories need concern us. Aristotle says that if the conclusion is converted and one premiss remains, it is necessary that the other premiss be 'destroyed' (*An. Pr.* 59b3). In a purely semantic setting if the contradictory of the conclusion and one of the premisses are true, it is necessary that the other premiss be false. For, as Aristotle notes, if that premiss were true, the conclusion would have to be true (*An. Pr.* 59b5). If '*P, Q* so *R*' is a valid syllogism, then $\neg Q$ must be a semantic consequence of $P, \neg R$. But Aristotle is making more than a purely semantic point. Aristotle shows that the syntactic structure of the syllogistic is such that $\dfrac{P,Q}{R}$ is a formal syllogistic inference in one of the three figures if and only if $\dfrac{P, \neg R}{\neg Q}$ is;[26] for example, each of the inferences $\dfrac{Aab \; Abc}{Aac}$ (*Barbara*), $\dfrac{Abc \; Oac}{Oab}$ (*Baroco*), and $\dfrac{Oac \; Aab}{Obc}$ (*Bocardo*) is related in this fashion. Let us call this the *conversion property* of the formal syllogistic. The upshot of this is that within the confines of the syllogistic, for every *per impossibile* syllogism of a conclusion there exists a direct deduction from the same premisses (cf. *An. Pr.* B14,

---

[26] Strictly speaking, *Darapti* and *Felapton* are exceptions to this statement, but only because of Aristotle's refusal to recognize subaltern moods: see Patzig, *Aristotle's Theory of the Syllogism*, pp. 152–3. See also, J. N. Keynes, *Studies and Exercises in Formal Logic*, section 266.

62b38–63b17; A29, 45a23–b21). *Per impossibile* syllogisms are similar to conversion, says Aristotle, differing only in that (i) in a conversion, one converts an already formed syllogism with both premisses assumed; (ii) in a *per impossibile* syllogism there is no prior agreement to the contradictory of the derived falsehood, but it is clear that it is true (*An. Pr.* B11, 61a21–25). What are these differences? A *per impossibile* syllogism may be of the form

(PI₃)   *P*, suppose *Q*; so *R*; but ⌐*R*; therefore ⌐*Q*.

A full conversion is of the form

(C)   *P*, *Q* so *R*, thus ⌐*R*, *P* so ⌐*Q*.

Here the use of the word 'so' signifies a formally valid syllogistic inference from premisses to conclusion. The final inference in both (PI₃) and (C) is to the same conclusion ⌐*Q*, and is from the same premisses ⌐*R*, *P*. The difference between (PI₃) and (C) is, first, in the *per impossibile* syllogism *Q* is explicitly supposed and thus isolated as the premiss to be overthrown if a falsehood is derived. Conversion proceeds, as a five-finger mathematical exercise, deriving the negations of each of the original premisses in turn, without any specific regard for argumentative role. Second, *per impossibile* syllogisms have an essential semantic component. The final inference in the *per impossibile* syllogism depends upon the belief that if '*P*, *Q* so *R*' is a valid syllogistic inference then ⌐*Q* is a consequence of ⌐*R* and *P*. The final inference is not one that has been isolated as syntactically valid, but is semantically guaranteed. However, had one thought to use ⌐*R* as a premiss in conjunction with *P*, one could have derived ⌐*Q* directly. Thus there is, within the confines of the syllogistic, never any point in employing a *per impossibile* strategy unless one has not antecedently realized from which premisses a conclusion may be derived. This is why in a *per impossibile* syllogism there is no prior agreement to the contradictory of the derived falsehood. If there were then there would be no need to use a *per impossibile* syllogism: one could deduce the conclusion directly. Yet it must be clear, for the success of the *per impossibile* strategy, that one has derived a falsehood or, equivalently, that its contradictory is true. For otherwise one could not go on to prove the contradictory of the supposition. Thus the contradictory of the derived falsehood must have been available as a potential premiss: though it is not agreed on beforehand, it must be clear that it is true.

The conversion property guarantees that, within the confines of the syllogistic, the only difference between *per impossibile* and direct syllogisms is one of argumentative structure. The *per impossibile* syllogism does not provide a method for deducing conclusions which could not be deduced by direct means. Since direct and *per impossibile* syllogisms use the same terms to deduce a conclusion (*An. Pr.* A29, 45a23–36), there is not just an abstract guarantee of the existence of a direct syllogism of any conclusion deduced by a *per impossibile* syllogism: the *per impossibile* syllogism actually furnishes the premisses from which the conclusion can be deduced directly. Given a *per impossibile* syllogism, if one changes the derived falsehood into its contradictory one can, in conjunction with the syllogistic premiss that was not supposed, directly deduce the conclusion of the *per impossibile* syllogism (*An. Pr.* A29, 45b4–8; B14). Thus the study of *per impossibile* syllogisms can be, for Aristotle, little more than part of an investigation into the role of supposition in argument. This is borne out by the contrasts Aristotle draws between direct and *per impossibile* proofs.

Direct proofs differ from *per impossibile* proofs, first, in that the former begin with two premisses assumed to be true, whereas the latter posit one premiss that they intend, ultimately, to refute (*An. Pr.* B14, 62b29–35). In a *per impossibile* syllogism one assumes one premiss and supposes the other to be true, while suspecting that it is false (*An. Pr.* A29, 45b8–10). That is the point of employing a *per impossibile* technique. So one difference between direct and *per impossibile* proofs is a difference of attitude toward the initial premisses.

Second, in a direct proof it is not necessary to know the conclusion nor to suppose beforehand that it is true or false, while in a *per impossibile* syllogism one must suppose beforehand that the directly deduced conclusion is not true (*An. Pr.* B14, 62b35–37). One cannot describe a *per impossibile* syllogism in abstraction from the epistemic state of those constructing it. A direct syllogism may be described in an epistemic vacuum. One may or may not know the premisses and one may or may not use a knowledge of the premisses to gain knowledge of the conclusion. Only when outlining what it is about a direct deduction that makes it a proof is one forced to describe an epistemic relation to the deduction. By contrast one must acknowledge an epistemic element in a *per impossibile* syllogism even *qua* deduction. One must recognize that the syllogistically inferred conclusion is false. This is so whether one is describing a *per impossibile* syllogism or a *per impossibile* proof. Even if one is only describing a syllogism it must nevertheless be assumed that only one of the premisses is being supposed – and, by contrast, that the other is known and asserted to be true – and that the derived conclusion is known to be false. Otherwise one cannot explain why the particular inferences that occur in a *per impossibile* syllogism are made. Thus one would expect Aristotle to pay little attention to the distinction between *per impossibile* syllogisms and *per impossibile* proofs. For the description of the *per impossibile* syllogism alone demands recognition of the argumentative context in which it is set in a way that a direct deduction does not. The line between a *per impossibile* syllogism and a *per impossibile* proof must be thin.

The only significant difference between *per impossibile* and direct syllogisms lies in the forced acknowledgement of argumentative role in the description of a *per impossibile* syllogism. This ultimately explains why Aristotle is not bothered by the inability of the syllogistic to express such arguments. I have already argued that Aristotle could not give an analysis of syllogistic consequence. For Aristotle's programme it is crucial that all imperfect inferences are perfectible: were the means of perfection inadequate to reduce all imperfect syllogisms, Aristotle would have had to devise an analysis of the concept of logical consequence which would justify treating a certain non-perfectible inference as valid. Since Aristotle explicitly warns against attempting to reduce *per impossibile* syllogisms (*An. Pr.* A44), one might think that the *per impossibile* syllogism would pose the recalcitrant imperfect inference that, by its imperfectibility, would topple the entire Aristotelian edifice. One might thus be led to wonder why Aristotle does not discuss the foundation of our belief that inference by a *per impossibile* syllogism is valid. If one is to argue validly, one must do more than make valid inferences, one must make inferences that are known to be valid. Not all knowledge is explicit: for obviously valid inferences we may not be able to say in what our knowledge of their validity consists. Yet we can simply see the truth of the conclusion as flowing directly from the truth of the premisses: e.g. from *Aab* and *Abc* it follows obviously that *Aac*. With a *per impossibile* argument, one simply infers from the derivation of a contradiction to the contradictory of one of the premisses. It is difficult to see in what one's knowledge of the truth of this statement consists. How does one know that the inference is valid? One certainly does not see its truth as directly built up from the truth of its premisses. Further, if a proof is supposed to enable one to recognize the explanation of the conclusion as the explanation (*An. Pst.* A2), how could a *per impossibile* argument ever be considered a proof?

If, however, one confines oneself to the formal syllogistic, these problems do not arise. Given a *per impossibile* syllogism in the language of the syllogistic –

P, suppose *not-Q* so *R*; but *not-R*; therefore *Q*

– the two ultimate premisses of argument, *P* and *not-R*, will be the premisses from which one can directly deduce *Q*. Thus the problem of one's knowledge of the validity of a *per impossibile* syllogism is reduced to that of our knowledge of the validity of a direct inference. One is never led by a *per impossibile* syllogism to a conclusion that cannot be deduced directly. One can see why Aristotle need not be bothered by the syllogistic's inability fully to formalize hypothetical syllogisms. For any *per impossibile* syllogism there is a corresponding direct syllogism which can be formalized; other hypothetical syllogisms may not be formalizable but they are not, strictly speaking, deductions at all. That fragment which is a deduction can be formalized. The claim that the syllogistic is adequate for the expression of all syllogisms (*An. Pr.* A23) is not threatened by hypothetical syllogisms. Since the *per impossibile* syllogism contains the premisses of a direct syllogism, in so far as it is possible for the one to embody the cause or explanation of the conclusion, so can the other.

Further, the *per impossibile* proof does not appear to be a genuinely alternative mode of proof. Within the syllogistic it seems no more than a technique of searching for premisses. If one wishes to prove a conclusion *Q*, which one does not know how to prove directly, one looks for any premiss *P* which one knows and which in conjunction with *not-Q* can be used to derive a known falsehood *R*. The contradictory of the known falsehood, *not-R*, will be the premiss needed to deduce *Q* directly. Thus when Aristotle comes to criticize proof *per impossibile*, in *Posterior Analytics* A26, all he can say is that the premisses which are prior in nature – those from which the conclusion can be proved directly – are not sufficiently familiar to us. The need for proof *per impossibile* arises from the fact that we are not born knowing the structure of the universe but must learn it. This we do by moving from experience of particulars to universals. Precisely because the direction of knowledge-acquisition is the reverse of the direction of cause in nature, what is familiar to us may not be what is prior in nature (*An. Pst.* A2, 71b33ff). Proof *per impossibile* is useful when our knowledge does not reflect the structure of the universe. It is a method not just for proving a conclusion, but of searching for the proper premisses from which a direct proof, embodying the cause (or explanation) can be formed. It is a method for bringing the structure of our knowledge into harmony with the structure of the universe.

4

Invalid inferences

A pair of premisses is *syllogistically sterile* if it has no syllogistic consequence. For every pair of premisses in the three figures Aristotle shows either that they are the premisses of a syllogism or that they are syllogistically sterile (*An. Pr.* A4–6). The proof of sterility of every premiss-pair that is not shown to be the premiss-pair of a syllogism is essential to Aristotle's programme: it is a test of the adequacy of the means of perfection. Were premiss-pairs not exhaustively partitioned, one would not know whether the means of perfection so far employed were sufficient to perfect all the imperfect syllogisms.

Since a syllogistic consequence follows of necessity from the premisses, to establish sterility one must prove a certain possibility. That is, one must show that it is possible for the premisses of the form in question to be true without any syllogistic conclusion, linking the major and minor terms in the prescribed order, being true.

The first premiss-pair Aristotle proves sterile is *Aba*, *Ecb* in the first figure.

> 'But if the first term belongs to all the middle, but the middle to none
> of the last term, there will be no syllogism in respect of the extremes;
> for nothing necessary follows from the terms being so related; for it is
> possible that the first should belong to all or none of the last, so that
> neither a particular nor a universal conclusion is necessary. But if there
> is no necessary consequence, there cannot be a syllogism by means
> of these premisses. Terms of belonging to all: animal, man, horse;
> terms of belonging to none: animal, man, stone.' (*An. Pr.* A4, 26a2–9)

Why is it that if it is possible for the major term to belong to all or none of the minor term then nothing necessarily follows? According to Ross and Kneale, if one can find terms *a*, *b*, *c*, such that *Aba* and *Ecb* are true and *Aca* is also true, then the possibility of the first two premisses having a negative first-figure consequence – either universal or particular – is eliminated. For example, since (i) the sentences 'All men are animals', 'No man is a horse', 'All horses are animals' are all true; and (ii) the sentences are of the form, respectively, *Aba*, *Ecb*, *Aca*, it follows that *Aba* and *Ecb* could not be the premisses of a syllogism with a negative conclusion, *Eca* or *Oca*. Similarly, if one can find terms *a*, *b*, *c*, such that the premisses *Aba* and *Ecb* are true and *Eca* is also true, then the possibility of the premisses of this form having an affirmative conclusion, whether particular or universal, is eliminated. Since (i) 'All men are animals', 'No man is a stone' and 'No stone is an animal' are all true; and (ii) these sentences are, respectively, of the form *Aba*, *Ecb*, *Eca*, it follows that *Aba* and *Ecb* could not necessitate an affirmative conclusion, *Aca* or *Ica*. The elimination of these two possibilities ensures that premisses of the form *Aba* and *Ecb* have no syllogistic consequence. Aristotle's procedure in this passage is simply to present two sets of concrete terms such that the premisses that can be constructed out of either set are actually true and of the form *Aba* and *Ecb*, while the actual relation between the extremes in the first set is universal affirmative and the actual relation between the extremes in the second set is universal negative.[1] Aristotle's method is to show that premiss-pairs are sterile rather than prove that specific moods are invalid. Given that a single proof of sterility shows, by implication, that four distinct moods are invalid, proving sterility is a far more economical procedure than proving invalidity.[2]

Consider the following argument: Actual states of affairs are *a*

---

[1] See Ross, *Aristotle's Prior and Posterior Analytics*, pp. 28–9; W. & M. Kneale, *The Development of Logic*, p. 75. Note that the sterility proof does not eliminate the possibility of the premiss-pair having any semantic consequence. It only eliminates the possibility of the premisses having a syllogistic consequence, linking the major and minor terms in the prescribed order. For example, the pair *Aba*, *Ecb* have no syllogistic consequence, but they do have a semantic consequence *Oac*. Aristotle's procedure does not eliminate this possibility because the major term *a* is functioning as the subject and the minor term *c* is functioning as the predicate. Remarkably, Aristotle notices this (29a19–29) but he expresses himself not by recanting and allowing that *Aba*, *Ecb* do after all form the premisses of a syllogism, but rather he says one *gets* a syllogism (γίνεται συλλογισμός) if one converts the premisses (29a23, 29a27). That is, if one converts both premisses one forms the premisses *Iab*, *Ebc* which are the premisses of a first figure syllogism (*Ferio*) with the conclusion *Oac*. Aristotle thus does not simply overlook the so-called fourth figure: he positively refuses to recognize it. (Cf. Patzig, *Aristotle's Theory of the Syllogism*, pp. 55, 168–83.)

[2] Aristotle employs two other methods of proving sterility. One is a deviant counter-example, technique, employed at 26a39–b14; for a discussion of which see Ross, *Aristotle's Prior and Posterior Analytics*, p. 304; cf. Patzig, *Aristotle's Theory of the Syllogism*, p. 178. The other is exemplified in Aristotle's proof at 26b14–19 that the pair *Aba*, *Ocb* is sterile. The argument is that (1) if *Aba*, *Ocb* had a syllogistic consequence *Xca*, then *Aba*, *Ecb* would have *Xca* as a consequence as well. But (2) *Aba*, *Ecb* was proved by counterexamples to be sterile (*An. Pr.* 26a2). Therefore (3) *Aba*, *Ocb* is sterile. This method of proof established the sterility of *Aba*, *Ocb* via the sterility of *Aba*, *Ecb* which was in turn proved by the standard appeal to counterexamples. Thus this method, which proves the sterility of a premiss-pair containing a particular premiss on the basis of the sterility of a premiss-pair containing an appropriate universal premiss, depends ultimately on the use of counterexamples. Cf. e.g. *An. Pr.* 27b12–23; 28b22–31; 28b38–29a6. (Cf. Patzig, *Aristotle's Theory of the Syllogism*, pp. 177–81.)

fortiori possible ones. Since we can be directly confronted with an actual state of affairs, we can be sure that that state is possible. *What is* is an epistemic paradigm of *what may be*: we can be certain that actual states of affairs with which we are directly confronted are possible. Thus Aristotle's proof of the possibility of certain predicational relations by appeal to actual predicational relations is a model for proving possibility. While there may be other ways to prove a premiss-pair sterile, Aristotle's use of actual counterexamples is a completely adequate method.

Peter Geach does not agree. He has objected to the entire Aristotelian approach of using counterexamples to establish syllogistic sterility.[3] Rejecting the premiss-pairs Oba, Ecb and Iba, Ecb Aristotle says

> 'Again if b belongs to no c, and a belongs to some b or does not belong or does not belong to all, there will not be a syllogism. Take the terms white-horse-swan; white-horse-raven.' (*An. Pr.* 26a36–39)

The first set of terms is supposed to show that while some horses are white and not all horses are white, all swans are white. But Aristotle was wrong about the colour of swans; they are not all white. So, Geach argues, 'the refutation fails in this instance, and is it not unworthy of logic to have to worry about black swans turning up, even if they never do?' The problem is not that of black swans turning up so much as that of *having to worry* about black swans turning up, *even if they never do.* The source of Geach's complaint is that a counterexample from any specific discipline – whether from botany, geology, physics or theology – will only show *that* an inference is invalid, not why. We must worry about our counterexample being overthrown because we do not know why the inference is invalid and thus the counterexample provides our only grounds for thinking that it is invalid.

Geach credits Saccheri with overcoming this difficulty 'by constructing, for each invalid mood, a counter-example belonging to logic itself'. Suppose, for example, one wishes to prove $\dfrac{Aba \quad Ecb}{Oca}$ invalid. One can construct, using second intention terms, the following syllogism S:

All instances of *Barbara* are valid	No instance of $\dfrac{Aba \quad Ecb}{Oca}$ is an instance of *Barbara*

Not all instances of $\dfrac{Aba \quad Ecb}{Oca}$ are valid

[3] Geach, *Logic Matters*, pp. 289–301. See especially pp. 298–9.

This syllogism is itself an instance of $\frac{Aba \quad Ecb}{Oca}$. As Geach correctly points out, even if this particular syllogism is valid, one cannot conclude that $\frac{Aba \quad Ecb}{Oca}$ is a valid form. For while every instance of a valid form is valid, not every instance of an invalid form need be invalid. Some instance of an invalid form may be valid because it is *also* an instance of a valid form. For instance,

$$\frac{\text{All men are men} \qquad \text{All men are men}}{\text{All men are men}}$$

is a valid instance of the invalid form $\frac{Abc \quad Aac}{Aab}$, but is also a valid instance of the valid form $\frac{Abb \quad Abb}{Abb}$. So one must argue as follows:

(1) If the syllogism S is valid, then since the premisses are true, the conclusion must be true. So some instance of $\frac{Aba \quad Ecb}{Oca}$ must not be valid. Thus the figure itself is invalid. (2) If, however, the syllogism S is invalid, then since it itself is of the form $\frac{Aba \quad Ecb}{Oca}$ this form must be invalid. Note that, as the argument has been formulated, it is misleading to say that one has constructed 'a *counter-example* belonging to logic itself', since no particular instance of $\frac{Aba \quad Ecb}{Oca}$ has been convicted of invalidity. One is thus faced with the following problem. If, on the one hand, S is a valid syllogism, then it seems to prove the existence of *some other* syllogism of the form $\frac{Aba \quad Ecb}{Oca}$ that is invalid. The proof is non-constructive, failing to provide an instance of the syllogism which is convicted of invalidity. If, on the other hand, S is invalid, then both its premisses and conclusion are true. Of course, invalid inferences may have instances in which both premisses and conclusion are true. But, given only an inference with true premisses and true conclusion, can one be confident that one will see why the inference is invalid?

Geach would have done well to stick more closely to Saccheri's actual procedure in the *Logica Demonstrativa*, which only appeals to syntactic facts about the syllogistic inferences.[4] Consider, in the manner

---

[4] See Hieronymo Saccherio, *Logica Demonstrativa, Theologicis, Philosophicis & Mathematicis Disciplinis accommodata*, e.g. pp. 81–3.

of Saccheri, the syllogism S':

$$\frac{\text{All instances of } Barbara \text{ are first figure syllogisms} \qquad \text{No instance of } \dfrac{Aba \quad Ecb}{Oca} \text{ is an instance of } Barbara}{\text{Not all instances of } \dfrac{Aba \quad Ecb}{Oca} \text{ are first figure syllogisms}}$$

This is obviously a counterexample, since it is of the form $\dfrac{Aba \quad Ecb}{Oca}$

and has true premisses and a false conclusion. This counterexample is derived from the theory of the syntax of the syllogistic. One may, if one wishes, call this a 'counter-example belonging to logic itself' so long as one is not thereby misled into thinking that the counterexample reveals why an inference is invalid in a way that any other obviously invalid syllogism does not. Saccheri's own method is indeed ingenious, but it does not yield any special insight into the why of invalidity.

Saccheri's procedure, says Geach, is not necessary to remove what he sees as the defect in Aristotle's sterility proofs. For we may convince ourselves that a syllogistic inference is invalid using Lewis Carroll diagrams, and this does not require any actual interpretation of the term variables.

How do Lewis Carroll diagrams work? Consider, as a simple case, the invalid inference $\dfrac{Aab}{Aba}$.[5] To reveal the invalidity of this inference one first constructs the diagram:

ab	ab'
a'b	a'b'

The prime "'" after a letter is a sign of complementation: so that 'a''' can be read as 'not-a' and has as its extension the Boolean complement of a. One then fills in the box according to certain rules for each type of syllogistic formula. Underlying the procedure is the idea that one fills a box with an X if the truth of the premisses ensures that there is something in the extension of the terms or with an O if the premisses ensure

[5] Invalid syllogistic inferences require a slightly more complex diagram, the complexity of which is irrelevant to the point I wish to make. See Lewis Carroll (Charles Dodgson), *Symbolic Logic Part I, Elementary*, pp. 21–83.

that there is nothing in the extension. To test the validity of an inference, Geach has suggested that one try to represent the premiss(es) together with the contradictory of the conclusion.[6] If one can do this the inference is invalid; if one cannot, the inference is valid. So to test the validity of $\dfrac{Aab}{Aba}$ we first represent the premiss, according to Lewis Carroll's rules:

ab		ab'
X		O
a'b		a'b'

The X in the upper left-hand corner reveals that there are a that are b and the O in the upper right corner marks that there are no a that are not b. This is, according to Lewis Carroll's rules, the information contained in the premiss. The lower left-hand corner is unoccupied, so it is possible to fill it in with an X, which represents the contradictory of the conclusion, that some b is not a:

(*)

ab		ab'
X		O
X		
a'b		a'b'

Thus the inference is invalid.

An obvious advantage of Aristotle's method over this test is that it provides terms with which one can construct truth-defeating instances of all invalid moods related to the sterile premiss-pair. One is thus not merely convinced of the abstract possibility that the inference may lead from truth to falsity. This possibility would hold even if the inference preserved truth for all instances using the terms of one's language. Aristotle's method allows one to construct actual instances of the invalid inference, in one's own language, which are witness to its invalidity. This is an important advantage, for on what grounds does one believe that the rules for filling in a Lewis Carroll diagram will distinguish the valid from the invalid inferences? Is it not because the rules harmonize with our pre-existing beliefs about which inferences

[6] See Geach, *Reason and Argument*, p. 57.

are valid? Were there any serious question about the validity of $\dfrac{Aab}{Aba}$ a Lewis Carroll diagram would be of no help. Someone who believed in the validity of the inference might well represent the premiss in a diagram:

(**)

ab	ab'
X	O
O	
a'b	a'b'

Then since the lower left corner is occupied it is not possible to represent the contradictory of the conclusion: the inference comes out valid. And on what basis should one prefer Lewis Carroll's rules for filling in the diagram rather than this man's? One might object, 'Look here, there is nothing in the premiss which says that no *b* is not an *a*', which there would have to be if the rules for *Aab* included putting a O in the lower left corner. But this objection does little more than state that we do not find the inference valid. One who 'saw' the inference as valid might reply by insisting that when he filled in (**) he was proceeding according to rules which only put in information contained in the premisses. We may feel that we have only put in information contained in the premiss whereas he has put in more. But he may retort that when, for instance, we fill in the upper right corner with a O we simply assume the inference $\dfrac{Aba}{Eb'a}$ is valid. Even if the inference *is* valid, he may say, the information that *Eb'a* is not contained in the premiss. So when one fills in a Lewis Carroll diagram one is doing more than merely recording the information contained in the premiss: the rules for filling in the diagram reveal one's beliefs about which formulas follow from which. The man who fills in the deviant diagram (**) may believe that he has seen more about what follows from *Aab* than we have.

Or, to take a more mundane case, someone might object that when we fill in the diagram (*) by putting an X in the upper left-hand corner we simply assume the validity of the inference $\dfrac{Aab.}{Iab}$ This inference has in the past been the source of debate and confusion.[7] Someone who thought the inference invalid on the grounds that *Aab* is true in an

---

[7] *Cf. e.g.* Bochenski, *A History of Formal Logic*, pp. 365–7.

empty domain would believe that when we filled in the upper left corner with an X we not only put in more information than was contained in the premisses, but we begged the question by assuming the inference valid. This case is straightforward, since there is no reason to think that we could not locate the source of our disagreement. But it does make it clear that the rules for filling in and interpreting a Lewis Carroll diagram are useful because they are formulated in a context of general agreement about which are the valid and which are the invalid inferences. Geach is correct that we may convince ourselves that a syllogistic inference is invalid using Lewis Carroll diagrams. However, the reason for this is that the diagrams conveniently codify our pre-existing beliefs.

Geach's point might have been stronger if he had recommended that one convince oneself with Euler rather than Lewis Carroll diagrams. For Euler diagrams give a spatial representation of the extensions of the predicates which one can visualize.[8] The situation described by *Aab* is compatible with both Euler diagrams:

(i)

(ii)

The Euler diagram, it might be argued, enables one to see *why Aab* may be true and *Aba* false, in a way which the Lewis Carroll diagram fails. It reproduces in spatial extensions the analogous situation that would have to occur with respect to predicate extensions for an instance of

$$\frac{Aab}{Aba}$$ to be truth-defeating.

But even if one thus convinces oneself of the invalidity of the inference, on what grounds is one justified in being so convinced? Suppose one appeals to the actual spatial relations that exist in the diagram (i) as drawn. By giving the variables of the syllogistic formula the appropriate spatial interpretation, the actual spatial relations in the diagram are

---

[8] One then must put up with the inconvenience – which Lewis Carroll diagrams avoid – that none of the formulas '*Aab*', '*Iab*', '*Oab*' can be represented by a single Euler diagram. Thus one may have to draw more than one Euler diagram to show that a syllogistic inference is invalid.

supposed to show that the inference in question, under the normal predicate interpretation, is invalid.[9]

If one appeals to the actual spatial relations of the Euler diagrams, then one is not justified in attacking Aristotle's use of actual counter-examples *per se*: at most one can object to the type of counterexamples Aristotle employed. Why is this use of Euler diagrams superior to Aristotle's use of biology or general knowledge? If the logician *qua* logician ought not to have to appeal to the actual truth of premisses in proving invalidity (or sterility), the present argument will not help, for it demands appeal to actual spatial relations. Perhaps the superiority of the Euler diagrams lies in the fact that one need not worry about black swans turning up, even if they never do. However, Euler diagrams do not put an end to epistemic anxiety. One may not have to worry about black swans turning up, but one ought to worry about the type of surface on which the diagrams are drawn. If we draw an Euler diagram on a sheet of paper, it is convincing because we assume that the surface on which it is drawn has the same topology as a Euclidean plane. Our perception of boundaries, of interior and exterior spaces is governed by this assumption.

Suppose that when we drew an Euler diagram like (i) we unwittingly drew it not on a Euclidean plane but in 'Escher-space' which, from a Euclidean point of view, looks like a torus.[10]

---

[9] One can also use Euler diagrams to prove a premiss-pair sterile. Instead of using the term white-horse-swan, white-horse-raven to show *Oba, Ecb* sterile, one can, on this view, construct the diagrams:

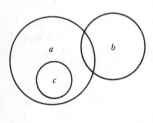
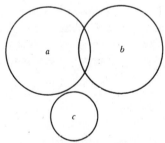

[10] Smiley suggested this example to me.

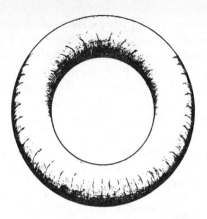

Were the line 'enclosing' *a* drawn around the 'hole' of the torus one would fail to enclose a proper subspace of *b*.

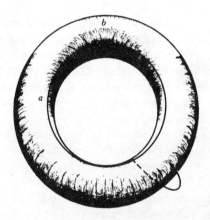

The topological structure of the torus differs from that of a Euclidean plane in that drawing a circle on it is not sufficient to guarantee that one has divided the surface into two distinct, disjoint areas.[11] So the Euler diagram actually drawn would fail to provide a counterexample to the invalid rule of conversion, and is it not unworthy of logic to have to worry about Escher spaces turning up, even if they never do? This

[11] The important topological fact about the torus is that it is not simply connected. If we draw the Euler diagram on a simply connected surface other than a Euclidean plane, e.g. a Euclidean sphere, it will divide the surface into two distinct disjoint areas.

envisaged failure to prove possibility by appeal to the actual is symmetrical to Aristotle's in that (*a*) the inference in question is invalid; (*b*) the alleged counterexample is not in fact a counterexample; (*c*) the alleged counterexample convinces one of the invalidity.

One might want to escape from this objection by insisting that one does not appeal to the actual spatial relations of the Euler diagram: rather, the diagrams are purely heuristic. The claim that the use of Euler diagrams is purely heuristic is ambiguous. The strongest interpretation of the claim is, I think, that the Euler diagram enables us to see how to construct actual counterexamples. That is, the Euler diagram in effect provides us with a rule for constructing counterexamples that invalidate the inference. For example, by studying Euler diagram (i) I can see how to invalidate $\dfrac{Aab}{Aba}$ in a domain of only two objects; for instance, the pen and pencil on my desk. I simply let '*a*' be 'pencil on my desk' and '*b*' be 'writing implement on my desk'.

Through this heuristic use of Euler diagrams one is, with Aristotle, brought back to the use of actual counterexamples to invalidate an inference. One cannot now quibble with Aristotle on the use of actual counterexamples *per se*, but only on the type of actual counterexample employed. Aristotle ran into trouble because he relied on a non-observational counterexample, the colour of all swans. One has far less chance of failing to appeal to the actual if one confines oneself to the writing implements on one's desk or, for that matter, the colour of swans which one has actually seen.

Further, Aristotle's sterility proofs do not merely provide counterexamples: they possess the same heuristic value as an Euler diagram. For when Aristotle presents sets of concrete terms, he also states what predicational relations they are supposed to exhibit. (E.g. the terms animal-man-horse are 'terms of belonging to all' (*An. Pr.* 26a8).) By recognizing the predicational relations that the counterexample is supposed to exhibit one can easily proceed to form other counterexamples. Aristotle's sterility proofs supply both the heuristic information of an Euler diagram and (except in one unfortunate case) an actual counterexample.

Even the unfortunate case may not be *that* unfortunate. There is no doubt that when Aristotle presented the terms white-horse-swan he thought he was presenting an actual case in which the major term is predicated universally and affirmatively of the minor. However, it does not follow that when Aristotle fails to present an actual case he has failed to prove a possibility. For Aristotle's counterexamples may serve functions other than being actual cases. As long as one can recognize Aristotle's *intention* that white-horse-swan exhibit a universal affirmative predication between the extremes, one can use the terms Aristotle gives to construct the diagrams:

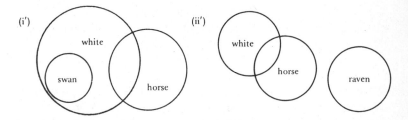

(i') white swan horse

(ii') white horse raven

One can take the diagrams to exhibit predicational relations which are witness to the sterility of *Oba, Ecb* even if one is mistaken about the actual extension of the terms used in the construction of the diagram. Thus, in the one case in which Aristotle fails to prove the possible by recourse to the actual, his method collapses into a variant of the method of providing Euler diagrams. That is, by recognizing Aristotle's belief that all swans are white, one can use the terms as variables and supply them with the extensions which it is believed they have. The failure is similar to that of drawing Euler diagrams in 'Escher space'. One can recognize the intention that the diagrams be drawn on a Euclidean plane and thus one need not worry about either black swans or Escher spaces turning up, even if they sometimes do.

A more abstract interpretation of the claim that the Euler diagram is purely heuristic is that it enables one to see that a certain relationship holds within the set theory of mathematical points. Just as one would not fail to prove Euclid 1–32 if the figure one drew on the blackboard did not actually have interior angles equal to two right angles, neither does one fail to prove the possibility of certain spatial relations even if the Euler diagrams one draws actually fail to embody them. By drawing the diagrams one comes to see that within a Euclidean plane, circles could be drawn that embody the requisite spatial relations. One is persuaded of a possibility, but not *via* a presentation of an actual case. This approach is supposed to free one from a dependence on the actual. However, what grounds are there for believing that the set theory of points describes a possible structure? One may not appeal to the existence of an actual structure, for such an appeal would land one squarely back with the very problem this approach is supposed to avoid. Denied appeal to the actual, one might try to show that elementary Euclidean plane geometry describes a possible structure by pointing to the fact that it is demonstrably consistent.[12] However, one must be cautious in moving from the fact that a theory is consistent to the assumption that it describes a possible structure. For suppose the consistency proof were model-theoretic (e.g. one shows that Euclidean plane geometry can be modelled within a richer solid geometry). Then one only shows that if one assumes that some other theory describes a possible structure one can model the original theory within it. Such a procedure is unhelpful, since it only shifts to a different structure the question of why one thinks a certain structure is possible. On the other hand, suppose that the consistency proof is proof-theoretic. Such a proof proceeds by analysing the structure of proofs and showing that for no sentence P of the language of the theory are P and $\neg P$ derivable from the axioms. One thus still needs an argument which moves from the non-derivability of contradictions to the existence of structures which are models of that system. Such an argument would be a completeness proof for the theory. For one way to prove the completeness of the axioms and rules of a theory T is to show that if a sentence P is not a theorem, then there is a model of the axioms of T and $\neg P$. But consider the form of a Henkin-style consistency proof: it *assumes* the existence of certain structures on the basis of which one can construct an interpretation which provides a model of T and $\neg P$. Again the problem is shifted but not resolved.[13] Further, a counterexample from set theory should hardly be satisfying to Geach. For it would not be a 'counter-example belonging to logic itself': it is as bound to a particular discipline as is a counterexample from physics.

In summary, someone who wishes to avoid Aristotle's use of

---

[12] Indeed it is even decidable. Cf. Alfred Tarski, 'What is elementary geometry?'; and *A Decision Method for Elementary Algebra and Geometry*.

[13] Benacerraf has raised the further problem of how knowledge of Platonic objects is possible at all ('Mathematical Truth'). Even if the set theory of points did describe a possible structure, how could we know it? It is doubtful that a proponent of this interpretation could answer this question by construing set theory non-platonistically. Putnam, for example, has argued that one should interpret set theory modally: one should view mathematics as making ontologically neutral statements of possibility and necessity. 'Sets if you will forgive me for parodying John Stuart Mill, are permanent possibilities of selection' ('Mathematics without foundations', *Philosophical Papers*, vol. I, p. 49). Sets are viewed as reifications of possibilities. To try to prove that certain spatial relations are possible by assuming the existence of a set-theoretic model would be, on this view, to assume the possibility one is trying to prove; albeit in an ontologically disguised form.

counterexamples by using Euler diagrams is faced with the following trilemma: either (1) he appeals to the actual spatial relations of the Euler diagram in which case he cannot completely avoid the danger that some appeal to the actual may fail. He differs from Aristotle not on the issue of using actual counterexamples, but only on the type of actual counterexamples it is safe to use. Or (2) the Euler diagrams are taken as purely heuristic, but they function as tools for constructing actual counterexamples. The usefulness of the Euler diagram depends upon the facility with which it enables one to construct an actual counterexample. One has not left actual counterexamples behind: they are the foundations of this procedure. Further, in heuristic value, Aristotle's own sterility proofs are equivalent to the Euler diagrams. Or (3) the Euler diagrams are purely heuristic, enabling one to see that certain relations could hold in the set theory of points. Here one does not escape the problem of having simply to assume that certain structures are possible.

The Aristotelian proof of possibility moves from a contingent premiss – that certain predicational relations actually exist – to a necessary conclusion – that it is proved that certain predicational relations are possible. This may be the source of the disquiet that underlies the various objections to Aristotle's use of actual counterexamples.[14] Let P be a sentence expressing the existence of certain predicational relations. Then Aristotle's sterility proof moves from appeal to the actual instantiation of P to the claim that it is proved that $\diamond P$. Let us call such a proof *S5-acceptable*. An inference from P to $\diamond P$ is unproblematic: actual predicational relations are *a fortiori* possible. But how can one move from an appeal to the actuality of P to the claim that it is *proved* that $\diamond P$? This question conflates two distinct problems. The first is how, on the basis of this form of proof, we can claim that what has been proved is necessary. The second is how one could be justified in claiming that one had proved a possibility.

The first problem, over necessity, should not arise for anyone who finds the notion of contingent possibility incoherent. I do not know how to argue for iterated modalities in a way, which avoids heavy appeal to intuition. Given that caveat, I cannot make sense of the claim that a state of affairs is *logically* possible though it is possibly not possible. This is because I cannot see how a state of affairs genuinely might be logically impossible, yet fail to be impossible. The difficulty is

[14] Cf. e.g. Ross, *Aristotle's Prior and Posterior Analytics*, pp. 28–9; Łukasiewicz, *Aristotle's Syllogistic From the Standpoint of Modern Formal Logic*, p. 74; Geach, *Logic Matters*, pp. 298–9.

compounded when, as in this case, the possible state of affairs happens to be actual. Here we must entertain the idea that a state of affairs which actually exists might have been logically impossible. The semantics has to be quite bizarre to satisfy both the claims (i) P and (ii) $\neg\Box\Diamond P$. To satisfy (i) P must be true in the actual world. To satisfy (ii), which is equivalent to $\Diamond\Box\neg P$, there must be a world w in which P is necessarily false. That is, in all worlds accessible to w, P is false. The accessibility relation of such a model appears artificial and odd. The actual world must have access to a world which does not have access to it. The concept of logical possibility is such that it should not be restricted by accessibility relations. If we wish to know what is possible, we wish to know what is true in *all* possible worlds. These remarks do not refute the thesis that there are logical possibilities which are only possibly possible. They do, however, shift the burden to those who believe in non-necessary logical possibilities to explain themselves.

What objection is there to regarding an $S5$-acceptable proof, of the type described, as a proof? The second problem, concerning proof, arises because the contingent premiss is not itself proved nor is it necessary or known *a priori*; and there is always a danger that one's appeal to the actual will fail. However, no form of proof is epistemically airtight. In, for example, an axiomatic proof, one must assume that the axioms are true and there is always the danger that one will be mistaken. If, on the one hand, one's objection to $S5$-acceptable proofs is based on the radical Wittgensteinian fear that no matter what one may do to safeguard one's appeal to the actual one may still fail, then a similar fear may infect any form of proof. We may thus 'divide through' by this fear. If, on the other hand, one's fear is more localized, then it should abate when one chooses actual cases for which the possibility of being misled is minimal. Aristotle failed because he used a theoretical belief about the colour of all swans. However, that failure could easily have been averted if he had appealed to an observational counterexample; e.g. the colour of all swans he had ever seen. Here it is not the appeal to the actual that should be questioned, but the type of actual case used. The source of the second worry is, I think, that while the conclusion – that certain predicational relations are possible – can be known *a priori*, the premiss – that certain predicational relations actually exist – can only be known *a posteriori*. However, *a priori* knowledge is that which one *can* come to know independently of experience: there is no reason why one has to.[15]

[15] See Saul Kripke, 'Naming and necessity'.

Indeed, there is no reason to believe that all possibilities can be known *a priori*. Peter Long has argued that the role of the actual in a proof of logical possibility *must always* be eliminable.[16] Long contrasts the role of the actual in demonstrating logical and physical possibility. For example, to prove syllogistic sterility one may appeal to the actual spatial relations of Euler diagrams. However, one could also simply describe the Euler diagrams or merely treat them as heuristic. By contrast, the role of the actual in the proof of the physical possibility of black swans could not be replaced by a drawing of a swan which was painted black:

> 'The role or function of the actual in demonstrating a logical possibility is essentially one that may be taken over by a picture or a drawing. In other words, a particular object or situation serves as a proof of a logical possibility through being used in a way in which a picture or a drawing may also be used. So it is not, as one might put it, by virtue of the actuality of the actual case that such a possibility is demonstrated by its means.'

Long maintains that since the role of the actual in a proof of logical possibility is essentially one that can be replaced, it is not in virtue of the actuality of the actual case that possibility is demonstrated.

At most Long has shown that the role of the actual in a proof of logical possibility may sometimes be replaced. For there is no reason to believe that an actual situation is always such that we could know, from the description, that it could be actual (or even possible). The actuality of a black swan convinces us that it is possible. Suppose, however, one were presented with a description of a black swan. One might not immediately be able to see whether or not such a thing is logically possible: that is, there will be nothing in the description such as 'this animal is black and white all over' which would immediately enable us to see that there could be no such animal, but what guarantee do we have that there is no contradiction hidden in the description?[17]

For many possibilities that we know simply by experiencing them,

---

[16] Peter Long, 'Possibility and actuality'.

[17] Imagine, for example, that modern science vindicated Aristotle by showing that the genetic structure of a swan was such that for a swan to be black there would have to be a gene at exactly the position which must be left vacant if the genetic structure is to be that of a swan. Thus to envisage the possibility of a black swan is to envisage the possibility of a particular gene being both present and absent from the same place at the same time.

there is no reason to believe that a description of the situation, which happens to be actual, would convince us even of its logical possibility. There would in many cases remain a suspicion that the description disguises a contradiction. Anything that is physically possible is *a fortiori* logically possible, but not conversely. Long himself admits that the actual cannot always be replaced in a proof of physical possibility. Yet one may learn, for example, that a black swan is logically possible via knowledge that it is physically possible. There is no guarantee that the logical possibility of a black swan could be known *a priori*.

Lukasiewicz also objects to Aristotle's use of counterexamples. His complaint is not with Aristotle's appeal to the actual, but with his use of concrete terms – e.g. 'swan', 'white' – in logic.[18] Instead, Lukasiewicz recommends rejecting invalid syllogistic moods axiomatically.[19] He takes two second figure moods –

<blockquote>'If Acb and Aab then Iac'</blockquote>

and   'If *Ecb* and *Eab* then *Iac*'

– as axiomatically invalid. On the basis of these axioms and two rules of rejection, Łukasiewicz is able to reject all other invalid syllogistic moods.

Lukasiewicz does not give any reason why one should not use concrete terms in logic. I suspect his objection derives from a confusion of formal logic with an uninterpreted formal system,[20] but as he gives no argument one cannot rise above the level of suspicion. One problem that might arise with concrete terms is that one's language might not be sufficiently rich to provide counterexamples for every sterile premisspair. However, even if one did suffer from a paucity of concrete terms, there would be nothing to hinder one from supposing the terms in one's language to have extensions different from the ones they actually have. Only if one did not know how to devise a counterexample to an invalid inference would there be serious trouble with the use of counterexamples. This is a problem which confronts the modern logician, not Aristotle. For he was able, using the methods of perfection and counterexample, exhaustively to partition all syllogistic premisspairs without even having to resort to a reinterpretation of the extensions of the terms of his language. In modern logic the task is not so

[18] Łukasiewicz, *Aristotle's Syllogistic*, pp. 96, 74.
[19] Łukasiewicz, *Aristotle's Syllogistic*, pp. 67–72, 96–7.
[20] See Chapter 1.

easy. By the Löwenheim–Skolem theorem, for any invalid inference in first-order logic, one can construct a counterexample to it in the domain of natural numbers. So, given that one accepts the natural numbers as an unproblematic structure, one knows that a counterexample can always be constructed to an invalid first-order inference, using natural numbers. For a particular inference, however, one may not know how to construct the appropriate counterexample. I am not arguing that counterexamples are the only method or even necessarily the best method for proving every inference invalid. I am only arguing that when, as in Aristotle's case, one has an actual counterexample at hand, that is as good a method of proving invalidity (or sterility) as any other.

Łukasiewicz's system of rejection is intended to be a mirror image of Aristotle's theory of perfection. But since he takes the syllogism to be a conditional, he misinterprets the perfection of a syllogism as the proof of a theorem from axioms. Rejection is supposed to be an operation opposed to Frege's assertion: 'We assert true propositions and reject false ones.'[21] In fact, the 'rejection of an invalid mood' amounts to no more than the assertion that the syllogistic inference corresponding to a given conditional is invalid.[22] Nevertheless, suppose one had an axiomatic system, similar to Łukasiewicz's, in which a few conditionals were chosen as 'axioms' of rejection on the grounds that the corresponding inferences were invalid. Suppose further that the rules of derivation were such that we could see that given a derivation that '(If P and Q, then R)' should be rejected, it followed that the corresponding inference $\dfrac{P, Q}{R}$ must be invalid. I would not wish to quarrel with anyone who actually wanted to use such a system; I would only want to maintain that such a procedure does not possess any significant advantage over a simple use of counterexamples.

First, consider the selection of 'axioms' of rejection. On what basis should a conditional be selected as an 'axiom' other than that it is easy to see how to construct a counterexample? Ross argued that instead of using counterexamples Aristotle should have simply appealed to the form of an invalid inference as the source of its invalidity. Aristotle,

---

[21] Łukasiewicz, *Aristotle's Syllogistic*, pp. 94, 71.

[22] More precisely, we reject a conditional either if it is a false sentence or if it contains free variables and there is a substitution instance of terms that turns the conditional into a false sentence (pp. 94–5). Thus, for Łukasiewicz, both the open formulas '*Abc* & *Eab⊃ Iac*' and '⌐ *(Abc* & *Eab⊃ Iac)*' are rejected. The reason is that (i) (*Σ*a) (*Σ*b) (*Σ*c) (⌐ *(Abc* & *Eab⊃ Iac)*) and (ii) (*Σ*a) (*Σ*b) (*Σ*c) (*Abc* & *Eab⊃ Iac*).

says Ross, 'would have done better to point to the obvious fact that the propositions "All B is A and no C is B" have no tendency to show either that all or some or no C is A or that some C is not A.'[23] This criticism assumes either that all valid inferences are obviously valid or that we know that the means of perfection we have thus far employed are sufficient to perfect all unobvious valid inferences. Aristotle refrained from either illicit assumption. Since the point of partitioning all syllogistic inferences into valid ones and invalid ones was to ensure that all unobviously valid inferences had been isolated and that the existing means of perfection were adequate, Aristotle wisely did not rest content with the fact that a premiss-pair had no tendency to show that a conclusion followed. Perhaps one might want to make the stronger claim that for certain obviously invalid inferences one can just tell immediately and *a priori* that they are invalid. This may be true, but I do not think that anything more is being claimed than that one sees easily and clearly how to construct a counterexample.[24] Even those of us who still countenance *a priori* knowledge are nevertheless happier when we are sure that that for which we claim *a priori* knowledge is in fact true. An asymmetry between validity and invalidity is that every instance of a valid inference is truth-preserving, but not every instance of an invalid inference is truth-defeating; indeed, as we have seen, invalid inferences may have instances which are also instances of valid inferences. Of course, one may select certain inferences as obviously invalid, and the obviousness of the invalidity may depend on its form; but what this amounts to is that for inferences of this form, it is easy to see how to construct a counterexample. Thus with the axiomatic technique one has not left counterexamples behind; they provide the basis for the selection of 'axioms' of rejection.

Second, given that we can easily provide a counterexample to an inference $\dfrac{P, Q}{R}$ the derivation of the rejected '(If P and Q, then R)' from the axioms would seem to be pointless. It would, in particular, be a mistake to think that the derivation provided a deeper analysis or explanation of the invalidity of $\dfrac{P, Q}{R}$ than does a simple counterex-

---

[23] Ross, *Aristotle's Prior and Posterior Analytics*, p. 29.
[24] Consider e.g. Łukasiewicz's axioms of rejection: '*Acb* & *Aab*⊃ *Iac*' and '*Ecb* & *Eab*⊃ *Iac*'. The inferences corresponding to these conditionals *may* be obviously invalid, but I do not see what the obviousness can consist in other than the ease with which we can see how to construct a counterexample.

ample.[25] Moving from truths to a falsehood can often be very boring: there may be no deeper explanation to give than that one has invalidly inferred a false conclusion from true premisses. Even if there were an explanation, a derivation in a calculus of rejection would not provide it. If the basis for choosing the axioms is the ease with which a counter-example can be constructed to the corresponding inference, then there is no reason to view the axioms as more basic than or explanatory of the theorems. The main value of such an axiomatic system lies not in its explanatory power, but in its ability to prove invalidity in those cases

[25] Consider e.g. Łukasiewicz's rejection of '*Abc* & *Eab*⊃ *Iac*' (pp. 96–7). In order that the reader may easily be able to compare this with Łukasiewicz's other derived rejections, I hereby adopt, for the remainder of this footnote only, the Polish notation Łukasiewicz uses. Rejected expressions are marked with an asterisk before their serial number. We are first given two axioms of rejection
 *(1) *CKAcbAabIac*
 *(2) *CKEcbEabIac*
and two rules of rejection
 (R1) If the implication 'If α, then β' is asserted, but the consequent β is rejected, then the antecedent must be rejected too.
 (R2) If β is a substitution of α and β is rejected, then α must be rejected too.
Then, by substituting *p/Iac*, *q/KAcbAab* in the logical truth '*CpCqp*' we get
 (3) *CIacCKAcbAabIac*
From (3) (1) it follows by (R1) that
 *(4) *Iac*
Substituting *p/Iac* in the logical truth '*CCNppp*' we get
 (5) *CCNIacIacIac*
But since we can replace *NIac* by *Eac*,
 (6) *CCEacIacIac*
But then by (4) and (R1)
 *(7) *CEacIac*
By the law of identity
 (8) *Acc*
Substituting *p/Acc*, *q/Eac*, *r/Iac* in the logical truth '*CpCCKpqrCqr*' and taking account of (8) it follows that
 (9) *CCKAccEacIacCEacIac*
But then
 *(10) *CKAccEacIac*
Substituting *b/c* we get by (R2)
 *(11) *CKAbcEabIac*
*(11) must be rejected because substituting *b* for *c* in *(11) we get the rejected expression *(10).
There is nothing in this derivation which provides a deeper analysis of why the inference $\dfrac{Abc \; Eab}{Iac}$ is invalid than does the simple use of counterexample: e.g. let *a*=stone, *b*=man, *c*=animal. Indeed, on the basis of the derivation, it is even less obvious *that* the inference is invalid than on the basis of the counterexample. E.g. perhaps there is an unnoticed invalid inference in the argument. It should be noted that the method of rejection is used in Łukasiewicz's solution to the decision problem (Łukasiewicz, Chapter V). However, I am not arguing that the method of rejection has no value, but rather that it provides no special insight into why an inference is invalid.

in which we do not know how to construct a counterexample. For then we could establish an inference as invalid even though we do not know in what ways we can be led by it from truth to falsity. However, in so far as it is fair to ask that a procedure show *why* and not merely *that* an inference is invalid, one is better off with the counterexample method than with an axiomatic derivation. For suppose one had a derivation that established the inference $\dfrac{P,Q}{R}$ as invalid, but was ignorant of how to construct a counterexample. Then one might be said to know that the inference was invalid: for we derived a rejection of '(If P and Q, then R)' according to a procedure we know to be trustworthy in allowing us to derive theorems of rejection only if the corresponding inferences were invalid. But if one did not also know how to construct a counterexample it would seem odd to say that one knew why the inference was invalid. For one would have been convinced by an abstract argument without having been shown how in a particular case the inference can lead from truth to falsity. A counterexample, by contrast, shows how one can be led by the inferences from true premisses to a false conclusion. This, I think is a sufficient explanation of why the inference is invalid.

An interesting counterpart to Aristotle's system of rejection (which it could be argued underlies Lukasiewicz's method of rejection) is as follows.[26] One first takes certain inferences to be obviously invalid. Then for a given inference $\dfrac{P,Q}{R}$ that is neither obviously valid nor obviously invalid, one tries to move from the premisses of an obviously invalid inference to its conclusion by a series of inferences such that each inference is either obviously valid or an instance of $\dfrac{P,Q}{R}$. If one can do this, then $\dfrac{P,Q}{R}$ is invalid. Such a procedure is ingenious and sound: if, to take an example from sentential logic, one could move from the premisses $S \supset T,\ T$ to the conclusion S by a series of inferences which included only obviously valid inferences or the inference in question $\dfrac{P,Q}{R}$, then $\dfrac{P,Q}{R}$ would be shown to be invalid.[27] Yet when,

---

[26] Suggested to me by Smiley.

[27] A procedure which is clearly unsound would be a process of filling in intermediate steps in an (unobviously) invalid inference by a series of obviously invalid inferences. Just because we can move from P and Q to R by such a series does not rule out the

as in the case of the syllogistic, one can easily construct a counter-example to every invalid inference, this procedure also fails to provide a useful alternative. Aside from the fact that it is much more difficult to invalidate a syllogistic inference by this procedure than by Aristotle's (the reader is invited to try), the difficulty is not endured for any valuable gain. For if, as has been argued, inferences are selected as obviously invalid because it is easy to see how to construct a counterexample, then this process does no more than provide us with an *extended* means of moving from true premisses to a false conclusion. Why bother with all this if one can provide a counterexample directly? This procedure would be useful in those cases in which one did not know how to construct an immediate counterexample to $\dfrac{P,Q}{R}$, but one could invalidate it according to this procedure. In such a case, the procedure would show us how a counterexample to an obviously invalid inference can be used to invalidate $\dfrac{P,Q}{R}$.

Our principal interest in invalid inferences is to discard them. Invalid inferences are interesting only in so far as they are difficult to discover or easy to misunderstand: hence the traditional interest in fallacies. Inferences for which one can easily provide counterexamples – for instance all the syllogistic inferences – can be discarded, as Aristotle discarded them, without further ado.

---

possibility that R is a consequence of P and Q. For all we know there may be another chain consisting solely of obviously valid inferences from P and Q to R. Or even if there is no such chain that may only be because not all valid inferences are perfectible.

5

Invalid proofs

How might a proof fail? This is not a question that has greatly worried the modern logician, for he does not take the notion of proof seriously. The painstaking work that has been done in modern logic is in the analysis of what it is to be a formal deduction. The further specification of what makes a formal deduction a proof has been conveniently and easily tacked on: a proof is generally defined to be a formal deduction in which all the premisses are axioms. But nothing more is said about what it is to be an axiom than that the formula occur on a list of axioms. One consequence of this is that, from the perspective of modern logic, a proof is invalid only if at least one of its inferences is invalid: there is no invalidity that is not ultimately the invalidity of inference. Aristotle, by contrast, tried to give an analysis of invalid proofs that as deductions are perfectly valid. The most notorious example of this is a proof that begs the question.[1] Aristotle's treatment of invalid proofs reveals an admirable concern for proof as something over and above a collection of valid inferences. In this chapter, after a preliminary discussion of the theory of principles, I examine Aristotle's critique of circular and question-begging proofs.

According to Aristotle, a proof proceeds from principles, which are themselves non-demonstrable, toward their consequences. Aristotle's argument for the non-demonstrability of principles is characteristically terse.

> '[Proofs must] depend on primitive non-demonstrables because [otherwise] you will not understand if you do not have a proof of them: for to understand that of which there is a proof non-incident-ally is to have proof.' (*An. Pst.* 71b26–29)

The danger Aristotle wishes to avoid is infinite regress.[2] If the only way to come to know a demonstrable statement (other than incident-ally) is through a proof of it and if principles are demonstrable, then any proof of finite length will depend ultimately on premisses that are not

---

[1] Keynes distinguished between a fallacy of inference and a fallacy of proof. Question-begging must be classified as a fallacy of proof. See *Studies and Exercises in Formal Logic*, p. 425; Hamblin, *Fallacies*, p. 33.
[2] Cf. *An. Pst.* A3, 72b5–15.

proved and therefore not known. This situation is absurd, for it is in virtue of one's knowledge of the premises of a proof that one can come to have knowledge of the conclusion. Yet if one attempts to provide a proof of all demonstrable premises one will embark on an infinite regress.

Aristotle could have resolved this dilemma without resorting to so strong a thesis as the non-demonstrability of principles. All that is needed to block the dilemma is that there be certain statements – principles – which it is *possible* to come to know in some other way than by proof.[3] If one merely assumes that principles can be known independently of proof, the problem of infinite regress does not arise. In the construction of a proof the regress terminates either when one reaches non-demonstrable principles or when one reaches premises which though perhaps demonstrable can be known independently of proof. In *Posterior Analytics* A3 Aristotle says that principles are necessarily non-demonstrable:

> 'for if it is necessary to understand the things which are prior and on which the proof depends, and it comes to a stop at some time, it is necessary for these immediates to be non-demonstrable.' (72b21)

All that is really necessary is that one not need a proof in order to know principles. The thesis of non-demonstrability is not generated by an inherent need within the theory of proof, but by Aristotle's assumption that for demonstrable statements there is a unique route to non-incidental knowledge. There is also proof-theoretic evidence for criticizing the thesis of the non-demonstrability of principles. Consider the following syllogism S suggested by Kripke:

All bachelors are unmarried males	All unmarried males are bachelors

All bachelors are bachelors

Arguments can be advanced to support both (1) that the conclusion can be known (non-incidentally) independently of the proof, and (2) that the syllogism S is a proof of a principle. The argument for (1) is that the conclusion is an instance of the law of identity *Abb*, which can be known independently of a proof, independently even of what *b* is. What grounds might there be for objecting that this syllogism is not a proof? One cannot object to the awkwardness of the syllogism, which allegedly proves a self-evident conclusion. The question at issue is

---

[3] Here and in the next paragraphs I am indebted to Kripke, both for conversations and for his written work on *a priori* knowledge in 'Naming and necessity'.

precisely whether there can be such 'awkward' proofs. Nor can one
seriously object to either of the premisses being a principle. The minor
premiss can be considered a definition of 'bachelor' and since it is a
definition, it is convertible (cf. *Topics* 102a18, *An. Pst.* 95a15). One can
thus come to know the major premiss independently of proof, just by
knowing that the minor premiss is a definition. The premisses can thus
be treated as principles.

A more substantial objection to regarding S as a proof is that the
premisses are not, as Aristotle insists they should be, prior to the conclusion. For if the conclusion as well as the premisses is a principle then
they are all primitive (*An. Pst.* 72a6). And a statement is primitive if
there are no statements prior to it. So if the conclusion of S is a principle
– and therefore primitive – the premisses cannot be prior to it. This
objection is not overwhelming. πρῶτος (primitive) is the superlative of
the comparative πρότερος (prior). Thus a premiss is primitive if it is
most prior; if no premiss is prior to it. For the various senses of priority
see e.g. *Categories* 12 and *Metaphysics* Δ11. From these analyses it
follows that P is primitive if there is no Q (i) that is either cause or
explanation of P; or (ii) of which knowledge is required if one is to
know P. Note that (ii) is a significantly weaker condition than commentators normally cite. Barnes, for example, says: 'But there is an
obvious analysis of "P is primitive" viz. "there is no Q prior to P", i.e.
"there is no Q from which knowledge of P may be derived".'[4] From
there being no Q prior to P it does not follow that there is no Q from
which knowledge of P may be derived. It only follows that there is no
Q of which knowledge is essential if one is to have knowledge of P.
This distinction is crucial to understanding Aristotle's theory of how
knowledge of principles is acquired. To assert that a principle P is
primitive is not, in itself, to assert that one *could not* come to have
knowledge of P through any other premisses Q. It only means that one
need not know any other premisses Q in order to know P.

A proof, for Aristotle, is a syllogism that produces unqualified
understanding of a conclusion (*An. Pst.* 71b17–19). Therefore, if one
can maintain that it is possible through S to gain unqualified understanding of the conclusion, one might be forced to weaken Aristotle's
requirement that the premisses of proof be prior to the conclusion. One
gains unqualified understanding of a conclusion if one can recognize the
explanation of the fact as the explanation and recognize that the fact
cannot be otherwise (*An. Pst.* 71b10–17). Perhaps one might object

---

[4] Barnes, *Aristotle's Posterior Analytics*, p. 99.

that this syllogism cannot yield such recognition since the conclusion is self-evident. However, the claim that the conclusion is self-evident is plausible only if it is interpreted to mean that it *can* be known independently of demonstration. That the conclusion is self-evident does not mean that the only way one can come to know it is by immediately apprehending it as such. One can imagine someone who on a particular occasion failed to recognize an instance of the law of identity. (Perhaps he was sleepy, not paying attention, just learning the language, unable to grasp such large words, etc.) However he knows the premisses and is able to work through the syllogism until he, perhaps, says, 'Ah, yes, of course, all bachelors *are* bachelors.' One cannot rule out the possibility of someone coming to know the conclusion on the basis of the syllogism. In such a case it seems reasonable to assume that in virtue of the syllogism he has learned to recognize the explanation of the fact as the explanation – after all, all bachelors are bachelors in virtue of being unmarried men – and to recognize that the fact cannot be otherwise – it follows from a recognition of the premisses as necessarily true. S, it appears, is a syllogism from which one may gain unqualified understanding of the conclusion: it qualifies as a proof. That the premisses are not prior to the conclusion reveals not that the syllogism is not a proof but rather that priority is too strong a relation to be imposed on the premisses and conclusion of proofs. There are two related ways in which this requirement may be weakened. One might insist that the premisses be either prior to or at the same metaphysical level as the conclusion, rather than strictly prior to it. Or, one could insist on strict priority, except in the case in which the conclusion of the proof is itself primitive, in which case one need only insist that the premisses also be primitive – i.e. at the same metaphysical level.

Is there a way to rescue Aristotle from this criticism? Given that principles need not be non-demonstrable, alternative translations of 'ἀναπόδεικτος' as 'not proved' or 'undemonstrated' provide some hope that one might be able to reinterpret Aristotle as making a weaker and more justifiable claim. Barnes notes that Sextus recorded two senses in which a statement can be ἀναπόδεικτος: (i) if it is undemonstrated; (ii) if it does not *need* proof.[5] The claim that the conclusion of a proof must depend ultimately on that which itself is not proved or that which does not need proof completely escapes the above criticism. In fact, throughout the *Posterior Analytics* Aristotle presents strong arguments to show that proof must commence with premisses

[5] *Aristotle's Posterior Analytics*, p. 99.

that are themselves not proved (*An. Pst.* A3, A10, A19–23, B7, B19). Nowhere does Aristotle present a strong argument that the principles of proof must actually be non-demonstrable. Unfortunately, this gambit is blocked in the opening moves. Aristotle clearly declares that to understand a demonstrable statement one must have a proof of it (*An. Pst.* 71b28. See the passage quoted at the beginning of this chapter). Having taken such a strong stand, Aristotle is forced to treat principles as non-demonstrable.

Aristotle's critique of circular proofs rests on his mistaken notion that principles are non-demonstrable. The circular demonstrator offers a different solution from Aristotle's to the sceptical problem of infinite regress. The circular demonstrator believes, as Aristotle does not, that all knowledge comes from proof, but he denies Aristotle's contention that the premisses of proof must be prior to the conclusion (cf. *An. Pst.* A3). Aristotle argues that there cannot be circular proof, for any such proof would violate the strict ordering between premisses and conclusion that the priority relation imposes (*An. Pst.* 72b25–32). However we have already seen evidence to doubt whether Aristotle is entitled to insist on strict priority. At least in the case of principles he should only demand a partial ordering between premisses and conclusion: that the premisses be prior to or at the same level as the conclusion. Given a series of interdeducible principles –

(*) $\qquad\qquad\qquad P{\vdash}Q,\ Q{\vdash}R,\ R{\vdash}P$

– one could not rule that any of the deductions is not a proof solely on grounds of priority. Within the confines of the syllogistic this situation could arise if one had principles *Acb*, *Aba*, *Aac* which, because they were definitions, one knew to be convertible (*Topics* 102a18). One could then form the only perfectly circular chain of inferences that can occur in the syllogistic (*An. Pr.* B5) –

(**) $\quad \dfrac{Acb\ \ Aba}{Aca}\ \dfrac{Aca\ \ Abc}{Aba}\ \dfrac{Aba\ \ Aac}{Abc}\ \dfrac{Abc\ \ Aab}{Aac}\ \dfrac{Aac\ \ Acb}{Aab}\ \dfrac{Aab\ \ Aca}{Acb}$

and each inference in the chain might be considered a proof.

Aristotle charges circular demonstrators with a specific fallacy of proof (*An. Pst.* 72b32–73a6).

> '[circular demonstrators] say nothing other than that this is the case if this is the case – and it is easy to prove everything in this way.' (72b34)

If someone works through a series of deductions such as (*) he has only inferred *P* from *P*. It is thus a mistake to detach the conclusion from the premisses and regard it as proved.

'. . . those who assert that proof is circular say nothing other than that if *P* is then *P* is. And it is easy to prove everything in this way.' (73a4–6)

Strictly speaking it is not easy to prove everything in this way. It is, for Aristotle, impossible to *prove* anything in this way. Nor is it even true that one can infer anything in this way. There is no reason to believe that every statement will have distinct consequences which in turn have that statement as a consequence. Within the syllogistic this is clearly not the case, a chain of the form (**) being the only truly circular deduction possible. Nevertheless, the point Aristotle is making is that in circular proofs which do exist one does not prove a conclusion but, ultimately, only infers it from itself.

Aristotle is attacking a straw man. A serious circular demonstrator may be concerned with more than deducing a statement from itself. Barnes links an interest in circular proof to an interest in the methods of analysis and synthesis in Greek geometry.[6] In analysis one takes a theorem one wishes to prove and proceeds to derive, by a process which is both obscure and controversial, premisses from which the original theorem can be deduced. The process terminates when one reaches geometrical axioms. Then in synthesis one reverses the process and proves the theorem from the axioms. The point of moving through such a circuit would not be to prove the theorem from itself, but to find the axioms from which it could be proved. Further, one may use a chain such as (*) not to deduce straight through the chain, but to deduce some principle from other principles. That the chain forms a circle only means that, from the point of view of deducibility, the question of which principle is deduced from which others is arbitrary. From an epistemic point of view the question is not necessarily arbitrary. Each deduction in any direction can be considered a proof of

---

[6] Barnes, 'Aristotle, Menaechmus and circular proof'. There is so little extant information on the method of analysis that Descartes actually suspected the Greeks of suppressing it. See Pappus' summary in I. Thomas, *Greek Mathematical Works*, II, 596–8. For the current controversy, cf. e.g. Robinson, 'Analysis in Greek geometry'; Mahoney, 'Another look at Greek geometrical analysis'; Cornford, 'Mathematics and dialectic in the Republic VI–VII'; Gulley, 'Greek geometrical analysis'; Hintikka and Remes, *The Method of Analysis*.

the conclusion, so long as the person constructing the proof knows the premises at the time he constructs it. Since every principle can be known independently of proof, every deduction could function as a proof. Different people may start at different places in the chain, depending on which principles they already know and which principles they do not yet know. One is relieved of the need to grasp all principles intuitively. There is thus an approach to circular proofs which escapes Aristotle's criticisms.

Aristotle links circular proof with the notion of question-begging. The charge of 'begging the question' arose in the context of Greek disputation. One speaker whose task it is to establish a certain issue may ask his opponent to grant him certain premises from which his argument may proceed. The speaker begs the question when he asks to be granted that for which he is supposed to argue.[7] In *Prior Analytics* B16 Aristotle attempts to shift the notion of begging the question from the realm of informal debate to the realm of proof.

'... since we get to know some things naturally through themselves and other things by means of something else (the principles through themselves, what is under them through something else) whenever a man tries to prove what is not self-evident by means of itself, then he begs the original question. This may be done by assuming what is in question at once; but it is also possible to make a transition to other things which would naturally be proved through the proposed question, and prove it through them, for example, if *P* should be proved through *Q*, and *Q* through *R*, though it was natural that *R* should be proved through *P*: for it turns out that those who reason thus are proving *P* by means of itself. This is what those persons do who suppose they are constructing parallel straight lines: for they fail to see that they are assuming facts which it is impossible to demonstrate unless the parallels exist. So it turns out that those who reason thus merely say a particular thing is, if it is: in this way everything will be self-evident. But that is impossible.' (*An. Pr.* B16, 64b34–65a9)[8]

Of the various ways one may beg the question, Aristotle distinguishes two broad categories. One *trivially* begs the question by directly assuming the proposed question (*An. Pr.* 64b39). A proof is *non-*

---

[7] See *Topics* Θ 13, 162b31ff for an analysis of how question-begging occurs in debate.
[8] 'γράφειν' (to draw) which is translated in this context (65a5) as 'to construct' could also be translated in this context as 'to prove'.

trivially question-begging if (i) the proof attempts to establish what is not self-evident by means of itself, but (ii) the conclusion is not directly and obviously imported into the premisses.

According to Aristotle, one has non-trivially begged the question when: (i) one has deductions of Q from R and of P from Q; (ii) it is 'natural' to prove R through P; (iii) one regards '$R \ldots$ so P' as a proof of P from R. When conditions (i)–(iii) hold it turns out, he says, that one is proving P by means of itself (*An. Pr.* 65a3). Why is this? Consider Aristotle's illustration of this type of begging the question: the case of those who construct parallel lines (*An. Pr.* 65a4ff). It is, of course, not evident from the text just what fallacy those who suppose they are drawing parallel lines commit. Heath, drawing upon a remark of Philoponus, guesses that the theory of parallels to which Aristotle refers depended upon the assumption that given any line one could draw another line in the same direction as the given line.[9]

Given a line BC, construct another line DE in the same direction as $BC \ldots$
Therefore DE is parallel to BC.

After describing the fallacy of assuming that '$R \ldots$ so $Q \ldots$ so P' is a proof of P from R, Aristotle says that this is what those who suppose they draw parallel lines do (*An. Pr.* 65a4). Thus the problem with this argument is that the 'natural' way to prove that one can draw a line in the same direction as any given line is to prove it by first proving that for a given line one can draw a line parallel to it and then show that to draw a line parallel to a given line is to draw a line in the same direction.[10] The only way one would be justified in supposing that one could draw a line in the same direction as a given line would be if one had already shown that one could draw a line parallel to it.

It was Aristotle's belief in the non-demonstrability of principles and his desire to give a formal analysis of question-begging that leads to the conflation of question-begging and circular proof. For if the only way to gain knowledge of a conclusion R is by a proof from principle P, then any deduction of P from R can be a movement from known premiss(es) to a conclusion only if R had antecedently been inferred from P. Thus the proof is, in a disguised form, only proving P by means of itself. For this analysis of question-begging to be plausible, it is necessary that the *only* way one could come to know that one can

[9] Heath, *Mathematics in Aristotle*, pp. 27–30.
[10] Cf. Frege, *The Foundations of Arithmetic*, pp. 74–5.

construct a line in the same direction as a given line is by a proof that one can construct a line parallel to that line. Aristotle's analysis depends upon there being a unique natural route to knowledge. But if principles are demonstrable one cannot rule out the possibility of there being a plurality of natural routes to knowledge. Though *a* natural way of coming to know that one can draw a line in the same direction as a given line is first to prove that one can draw a line parallel to a given line and then derive the notion of a line being in the same direction, to say this is the only way one could gain such knowledge is to impose unjustified restrictions on routes to knowledge.

To see this more clearly, consider the following example from set theory. Let P be the axiom of choice, Q be Zorn's lemma, and R be the well-ordering theorem. P, Q, R are provably equivalent.[11] If one were to regard the deduction 'R ... so Q ... so P' as a proof of the axiom of choice, why would such a proof beg the question? Presumably an Aristotelian would say that a knowledge of the premiss depends upon an antecedent knowledge of the conclusion: the well-ordering theorem is proved via the axiom of choice. Suppose, however, one mistakenly thought that the well-ordering theorem was true for reasons entirely independent of the axiom of choice. For example, suppose someone wrongly believed that there were only finite and denumerably infinite sets – perhaps he had never seen Cantor's diagonal argument – and came to believe the well-ordering theorem true by reflecting on the ease with which an ordering function could be defined for such sets. Such a person who used the deduction 'R ... so Q ... so P' would fail to prove the conclusion for he would mistakenly believe that he knew the premiss. But the source of his mistaken belief is not trivial. If asked to expand the proof he could have provided a deep and non-circular account of why the premiss is true. It defies our intuitions to say he is trying to prove a statement by means of itself – even if one should concede that the only way he could have come to knowledge of the premiss is through the conclusion. For he is correct in his belief that if his justification for believing the premiss had given him knowledge, he would have had a significant proof of the conclusion.

Furthermore, Aristotle's analysis of question-begging depends upon the assumption that the *unique* route to knowledge of R is by means of a proof of it through P. For if it were possible to come to know the premiss R independently of knowledge of the conclusion P, it would

[11] Cf. Jech, *The Axiom of Choice*.

be possible to use the deduction to arrive at knowledge of the conclusion. Suppose that one could motivate the well-ordering theorem directly, by reflection on the iterative conception of set (the cumulative hierarchy). For example, at each successor rank in the hierarchy (Ra_{+1}) all sets of the previous rank are combined *in all possible ways*. For a given set x that occurs somewhere in the hierarchy, one might think that one of the possible combinations of its members will well-order x. This motivation is unconvincing because we do not now have a developed understanding of *combination in all possible ways* or of the powerset operation.[12] However, one cannot rule out the possibility that with a more developed understanding of the powerset operation, the well-ordering theorem could be used in an informative proof of the axiom of choice, which itself has been the object of controversy. A defender of Aristotle might object that in such a case one would simply have been previously mistaken about the natural route to knowledge. The proper route to knowledge of the axiom of choice would have been shown to be by a proof from the well-ordering theorem and not vice versa. There is, however, no reason to believe that there is a unique natural route to knowledge. Leading set theorists, for example Zermelo, have found the axiom of choice self-evident and the proof of the well-ordering theorem informative.[13] The existence of an alternative proof need not diminish the value of the traditional one.

Though we cannot accept Aristotle's analysis of question-begging, we can at least recognize that, as an attempt to characterize invalid proofs, it is far superior to more recent analyses. It is a commonplace that Mill thought that all syllogisms begged the question. What is less well known, however, is that the fallacy he thought all syllogisms committed is not the fallacy Aristotle described as begging the question. For Mill, a syllogism begs the question because the conclusion expresses an 'assertion' identical to one expressed by the premises, albeit in a hidden form.

> '... there is no more important intellectual habit nor any the cultivation of which falls more strictly within the art of logic than that of discovering rapidly and surely the identity of an assertion when disguised under the diversity of language'.[14]

It is not that 'R ... so P' is taken to be a proof of P when in fact one's

---

[12] Cf. Boolos, 'The iterative conception of set'.
[13] Zermelo, 'Proof that every set can be well ordered', 'A new proof of the possibility of a well ordering'. See also, D. A. Martin, 'Sets *versus* classes'.
[14] Mill, *A System of Logic*, p. 184. See generally Chapters 1–3.

knowledge of R depends upon a proof of it from P. Rather it is that R and P are taken to express the same 'assertion', though in a way which may not be immediately evident. Although one may say of this case 'that those who reason thus merely say that a particular thing is if it is' (*An. Pr.* 65a8), the error is essentially different from that described by Aristotle. On the Aristotelian characterization begging the question occurs solely in virtue of an interdeducibility among statements and a mistake concerning the direction in which the deduction should be regarded as a proof. Aristotle does not require that the premiss and conclusion need express the same 'assertion'. From the point of view of characterizing a failure of proof, Aristotle's analysis of question-begging is much better than Mill's. Any proof whose premisses it is possible to know, without initially recognizing the conclusion to be true, cannot be treated as question-begging. For in such a case one could use the proof to gain knowledge of the conclusion. The plea that the premisses express the same 'assertion' as the conclusion is futile. Even if one allows the problematic thesis that two distinct sentences may express the same 'assertion', the possibility that someone who knows the premisses may construct the proof to learn the conclusion refutes decisively the contention that premisses and conclusion express the same 'assertion' – at least in any sense that is useful for characterizing question-begging.[15]

Not only does Aristotle attempt a general description of a proof that begs the question, but he also lists conditions applicable specifically to the syllogistic which are supposed to be criteria of syllogistic question-begging.

'If then it is uncertain whether a belongs to c, and also whether a belongs to b and if one should assume that a does belong to b, it is not yet clear whether he begs the original question, but it is evident that he is not demonstrating: for what is as uncertain as the question to be answered cannot be a principle [or starting point, ἀρχή] of a proof. If however b is so related to c that they are identical, or if they are plainly convertible, or the one belongs to the other, the original question is begged. For one might equally well prove a belongs to b through those terms if they are convertible. But as it is [i.e. if they are not convertible] it is the fact that they are not that prevents such a proof, not the method of proving.' (*An. Pr.* B16, 65a10–18)

---

[15] For detailed criticisms of Mill's position, see Dummett, 'The justification of deduction'; Keynes, *Studies and Exercises in Formal Logic*; Hamblin, *Fallacies*.

Even if one is not certain whether *Aca* or *Aba*, suppose one constructed the syllogism:

$$\frac{Acb \quad Aba}{Aca}$$

Such a syllogism, Aristotle remarks, cannot be a proof. For one does not know the premisses and so one cannot gain knowledge of the conclusion based on one's knowledge of the premisses. Aristotle proceeds to list three conditions such that if the failed proof satisfies any one of the conditions, then the proof begs the question (*An. Pr.* 65a14–16). What are these conditions? Two terms *b* and *c* *convert* if *Abc* and *Acb*. If two terms are identical, they are convertible, but not conversely: for example, 'man' and 'featherless biped' are convertible but not identical. If *b* and *c* are either identical or evidently convertible why should the syllogism be guilty of begging the question? Aristotle says that one could equally well have proved *Aba* through the same terms (*An. Pr.* 65a16). Aristotle appears to be giving a formal equivalent within the confines of the syllogistic of his general characterization of begging the question (*An. Pr.* 65a1–4) in which one deduces *P* from *R* when in fact *R* is naturally proved through *P*. If *b* and *c* are identical or convertible one can convert *Acb* to *Abc* and in conjunction with the conclusion of the syllogism, *Aca*, infer the other premiss *Aba*.

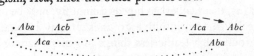

This type of convertibility of terms is a necessary and sufficient condition for circular proof within the syllogistic (cf. *An. Pr.* B5–7).

Such convertibility, however, fails as a criterion of syllogistic question-begging. Suppose, for example, that though *Aba* and *Aca* are equally uncertain, *Aba* is in fact a principle. This may be the case if one has not yet had enough inductive experience of particulars to comprehend the principle *Aba* (*An. Pst.* B19). The mere convertibility of *Abc* cannot be sufficient to guarantee that the syllogism begs the question. For on Aristotle's description, the deduction of *P* from *R* begs the question when *R* is naturally proved through *P*; i.e. when '*P* . . . so *R*' is an acceptable proof. Within the confines of the syllogistic the convertibility of terms is necessary for circular deductions. Yet if one is to regard any inference in the series of syllogistic inferences that constitutes the circular deduction as question-begging, then one must regard at least one of the inferences as the natural way of proving a conclusion from premisses. For it is only in virtue of the natural conclusion serving as a premiss in a deduction of a natural premiss that question-begging is said to occur. But in the inference in which the natural premisses (i.e. principles) occur as premisses and the natural conclusion occurs as conclusion, one of the premisses will be convertible since, by hypothesis, this inference occurs within a chain of inferences that constitutes a circular proof within the syllogistic. Thus this inference is, on the proposed criterion, question-begging; for it is possible to convert one of the premisses and in conjunction with the conclusion syllogistically infer the other premiss. But the inference is clearly not question-begging, since the natural premisses occur as premisses and the natural conclusion occurs as conclusion. Thus the proposed criterion of question-begging is inadequate.

Consider, for example, the syllogisms:[16]

(*a*) All featherless bipeds cannot fly   All men are featherless bipeds
                    All men cannot fly

(*b*) All men cannot fly   All featherless bipeds are men
            All featherless bipeds cannot fly

The possibility of constructing syllogism (*b*) does not provide sufficient grounds for concluding that syllogism (*a*) begs the question. The major premiss of (*a*), that featherless bipeds cannot fly, may be uncertain but thought to be true on intuitive grounds. It may be assumed on the intuitive ground that featherless things in general cannot fly. Yet the premiss is uncertain for it is uncertain what featherless bipeds are and thus possible that one's belief about featherless things in general might be falsified by a flying featherless biped. In conjunction with the minor premiss, that all men are featherless bipeds, one can infer that all men cannot fly. In such circumstances one may have failed to provide a proof, for one does not know the premisses and thus cannot come to know the conclusion on the basis of one's knowledge of the premisses. There is, however, no reason to believe that the syllogism begs the question. If one did know the premisses, then the syllogism could have been used as a valuable and informative proof of the conclusion – moving from a conceptual fact about the relation of feathers and flying through the empirical discovery that men have one of the properties (lack of feathers) to the conclusion that they have the other of the properties (lack of an ability to fly). Further, suppose that a non-human featherless biped was discovered, falsifying the belief that only humans were

---

[16] Here I am indebted to Hamblin's discussion of 65a10–18 in *Fallacies*, p. 75.

featherless bipeds, and the convertibility of the minor premiss; thus blocking the construction of syllogism (*b*). Why should that fact help rescue (*a*) from the charge of question-begging? And, more importantly, why should the mere lack of such a discovery, even if due to the fact that there are no non-human featherless bipeds, be sufficient to guarantee that the syllogism (*b*) begs the question?

Perhaps such questions as these motivated the third condition for begging the question – if of *b* and *c* 'one belongs to the other' (*An. Pr.* 65a15). On this criterion the terms need be neither identical nor evidently convertible. Thus the possibility of syllogism (*a*) being question-begging need not stand or fall with the discovery of a non-human featherless biped. Aristotle says that in such a case we would be technically prevented from carrying out a reciprocal proof, since convertibility of terms is a prerequisite, but the method of proof would still be question-begging (*An. Pr.* 65a17ff). Why? The third condition for a proof being question-begging appears perilously close to a description of a perfectly innocent inference in *Barbara*. One is given two formulas *Aba*, *Aca* of which one is equally uncertain and a premiss *Acb* which, in effect, is true. What reason is there for thinking that under these conditions the syllogism

$$\frac{Acb \quad Aba}{Aca}$$

begs the question? This is a perfectly acceptable inference in *Barbara* which fails to be a proof solely because at least one of the premisses is uncertain. Perhaps one should take Aristotle to be requiring not just that it be evident that terms convert, but also that it be *evident* that one term belongs to the other (*An. Pr.* 65a15). This interpretation permits a plausible description of how the syllogism can be construed as question-begging. For if it is *evident* that *Acb*, then if one simply assumes *Aba*, has one not, in effect, simply assumed *Aca*? If the minor premiss is obviously true, then in assuming the major premiss have we not really assumed the conclusion?

Such a description flies in the face of Aristotelian epistemology. Consider, for example, the syllogism

All scalene triangles are triangles	All triangles have interior angles equal to two right angles

All scalene triangles have interior angles
equal to two right angles

Suppose someone constructs this syllogism who, having never seen a proof of Euclid 1-32, happens to be equally uncertain of the major premiss and the conclusion. In simply assuming the major premiss he has failed to provide a proof for he does not know the premisses. Has he, however, begged the question by assuming the conclusion? Surely, Aristotle should not regard such a syllogism as begging the question. One could not believe that the syllogistic was a paradigm structure in which proof could occur unless one accepted that antecedently knowing that a property holds of a class of objects, one can come to know that the property holds of particular subclasses. In the spirit of *Posterior Analytics* 71a17–31: In knowing that all triangles have interior angles equal to two right angles Aristotle would say that one in a sense knows that all scalene triangles have the property – but in a sense not. One knows the universal truth expressed by the major premiss, but perhaps one has simply never thought of the property as applying to particular types of triangles (cf. *An. Pst.* 73b25–74b4). Certainly the proof of Euclid 1–32 is so general that one need not consciously consider the case of scalene triangles. To avoid the puzzle of the *Meno* – that one either learns nothing or what one already knows – one must accept that such obvious inferences can be used for knowledge-acquisition. Aristotle's criterion of a syllogistic proof begging the question should be rejected on epistemological grounds which Aristotle would himself endorse.

APPENDIX: A NOTE ON 'IGNORANCE'

There is a different and more straightforward way in which a proof may fail. Suppose that from premisses all thought to be true one has by a series of valid inferences deduced a conclusion known to be false. Then, of course, one does not have a proof of the conclusion, for at least one of the premisses taken to be true must be false. This is a problem which bothered Aristotle because he took proof to be an important means of knowledge-acquisition. The deduction of a conclusion known to be false, from premisses thought to be true, is a serious epistemological warning: for these premisses may be leading us to false beliefs which we do not recognize to be such.

Aristotle's theory of proof describes a process that moves in but one epistemic direction: away from principles, toward syllogistic consequences. In virtue of our knowledge of the principles and the use of rules of inference, known to be valid, one gains knowledge of the proved conclusion. The confidence with which a proved conclusion, for which there are no obvious independent grounds for its truth, is accepted as known is a function of the confidence one has that the process embodied in a proof is one in which knowledge is extended.

Are there ways of moving in the other direction? Suppose one has derived a conclusion known to be false. If the conclusion has been validly inferred, then it must have been inferred from one or more premisses that are false. Once a conclusion is recognized to be false, is there a systematic method for working one's way towards principles and isolating the points at which an error could have occurred? The direction of epistemic concern is here the reverse of that expressed by the theory of proof. The theory of proof is supposed to ensure that as one moves away from principles deriving consequences, one will never derive a false conclusion. The question posed, by contrast, assumes that somehow one has derived a false conclusion and asks whether there is a method for isolating the source of error.

'Ignorance' – at least the type of ignorance Aristotle called a 'disposition' – is error that comes about through deduction (*An. Pst.* 79b23). The question to which Aristotle addresses himself in *Posterior Analytics* A16–17 is: given that one knows oneself to be in a state of ignorance, is there a systematic method of searching for the source of one's error?

There is both a significant analogy with and a significant difference from a project that has exercised modern logicians: consistency proofs for formal theories. Hilbert showed that one could prove the consistency of a formal theory of arithmetic if it could be shown that no formal proof in the theory had '$1 \neq 1$' as the last line.[17] For since the system, if inconsistent, would allow the derivation of any conclusion, to show that there is some formula that could not be the last line of a formal derivation would be to prove consistency. Gentzen carved out such a proof of consistency for arithmetic. In a Gentzen-type consistency proof, the method is to inquire what structure a formal proof would have to assume if it were to have a particular conclusion such as '$1 \neq 1$'.[18] Gentzen's task, analogous to Aristotle's, was to work his way back from a conclusion (known to be false) toward the premisses from which it might be derived. He was guided in his search by a knowledge of the form any premisses in a formal derivation of that conclusion would

---

[17] Hilbert, 'On the infinite'.
[18] Gentzen, 'Investigations into logical deduction', 'The consistency of elementary number theory'.

have to assume. Consistency is proved by showing that for a particular obviously contradictory conclusion no formal proof could have it as a last line.

The difference is that the syllogistic deeply depends on a cousin of that rule of inference Gentzen called 'cut'. In his 'calculus of sequents', Gentzen interpreted the sequent

$$P_1 \ldots P_n {\to} Q$$

as $(P_1 \& \ldots \& P_n) \supset Q$, but he allowed there to be more than one formula on the right-hand side of the sequent: e.g.

$$P_1 \ldots P_n {\to} Q, R$$

Just as the antecedent is interpreted conjunctively, so the succedent is interpreted disjunctively: if P_1 and ... and P_n are true, then either Q or R is true. Cut was then introduced as a structural inference:

$$\frac{P_1{\to}Q_1, R \qquad R, P_2{\to}Q_2}{P_1, P_2{\to}Q_1, Q_2}$$

The formula R is 'cut out' and does not occur in the conclusion of the inference. The important point is that simply by looking at the conclusion '$P_1, P_2{\to}Q_1 \, Q_2$' one could gain no idea that R occurred in its derivation. This similarity between the cut rule and the familiar inference of *modus ponens* –

$$\frac{P, P{\supset}Q}{Q}$$

– should be clear. By looking solely at the conclusion Q one cannot determine the premisses from which it was derived. By contrast, consider the rule of and-introduction:

$$\frac{P, Q}{P \& Q}$$

From a knowledge of the conclusion one can recover the premisses from which it was derived, *provided* that the only way that '$P\&Q$' can occur as the conclusion of an inference is if it has been inferred by the rule of and-introduction. If it could also be inferred by *modus ponens* – e.g.

$$\frac{R, R{\supset}P\&Q}{P\&Q}$$

– then one cannot determine the premisses from which it was derived. Gentzen succeeded in proving (first order) arithmetic consistent by showing that for any derivation of a theorem of arithmetic there exists another derivation of the same theorem in which *modus ponens* – or, in the calculus of sequents, the related cut rule – does not occur as a rule of inference. All the inferences used in the new derivation are such that, from a knowledge of the theorem alone, one can determine to a remarkable degree the shape of the derivation and the premisses which occurred in it. By examining what a 'cut-free' derivation of '$1 \neq 1$' would have to look like, one can see that there is no derivation of it in arithmetic.

The syllogistic is a cut-saturated system: at every syllogistic inference information (the middle term) is sacrificed between premisses and conclusion. Given the conclusion of any syllogistic inference one cannot even determine the middle term of the premisses from which it was immediately inferred. The structure of the syllogistic, by contrast to a cut-free system, imposes relatively few constraints on the premisses from which a conclusion can be derived. Nevertheless there are some constraints. For example, a universal conclusion forces both the premisses from which it was derived to be universal, a negative conclusion requires one and only one negative premiss, a universal affirmative conclusion requires two universal affirmative premisses, any valid syllogistic inference requires at least one universal premiss. Aristotle takes advantage of the structural constraints that do exist in the syllogistic, in conjunction with certain non-structural constraints, in his attempt to isolate the sources of error in the derivation of a false conclusion. Though there are not sufficient constraints to make Aristotle's project a great success, there are enough to enable him to devise a proof-theoretic technique that could not be used fruitfully until the time of Gentzen.

If a validly derived conclusion is false, then at least one of the premisses from which it was derived must be false. This is a, slightly perverse, consequence relation, since every interpretation which puts the conclusion in a particular partition (the false sentences) will place at least one of the premisses in that partition as well.[19] Given that this consequence relation holds between sentences, is there any way of determining that it holds? One way is to use the inverses of valid rules of inference. For if the inferences are truth-preserving, their inverses are falsity-preserving. If the conclusion of a valid rule is false, at least one of the premisses must be false. Rules tend to be from a plurality of premisses to a single conclusion, since in the pursuit of truth one tries to isolate a single conclusion proved to be true. Thus given a derivation we may not be able to do more than isolate a field in which falsity must

[19] See Shoesmith and Smiley, *Multiple Conclusion Logic*, Chapter I, for an abstract definition of a consequence relation.

lie. This is trivially the case when we can do no more than isolate the premisses from which the conclusion was derived.

Nevertheless, since the inverse of each valid rule is falsity-preserving, there is a method of searching for falsity. An extended proof, within the syllogistic, is a series of two-premissed inferences; so given a false conclusion at least one of the two premisses from which it is immediately inferred must be false. This false premiss (or premisses) may itself be derived or it may occur as an illegitimate postulate. If the false premiss is derived then at least one of the premisses from which it is immediately inferred must be false. One can work one's way up a proof tree through the false premisses until one reaches a false premiss that is not derived. This is the source of error in the derivation.

A true conclusion, as Aristotle knew, can be derived from false premisses (*An. Pr.* B2–4). If in the course of a derivation false premisses yield a true conclusion, the danger of the falsity of those premisses infecting the conclusion of the entire derivation is effectively sealed off. The derivation will not be a proof, since not all the premisses are true, but the falsity of these premisses will not be responsible for the truth or falsity of the conclusion.

Thus to provide a method for locating the source of error in a derivation of arbitrary length, one need only concentrate on the structure of the immediate inference. In *Posterior Analytics* A16–17, Aristotle confined himself to syllogisms from which universal conclusions can be derived. Thus the problem Aristotle confronts is that one has derived a conclusion either of the form *Aba* or *Eba* which one knows to be false.

Since at every inference a middle term is sacrificed, one might expect that Aristotle's systematic study of deductive error would compensate for the loss of information between premisses and conclusion. This expectation is justified. *Posterior Analytics* A16 and A17 divide on whether or not the conclusion holds atomically. In *Posterior Analytics* A15 Aristotle explains that a predicate belongs or does not belong to a subject atomically if 'there is no middle term for them' (*An. Pst.* 79a35). That is, a sentence *Aba* or *Eba* is *atomic* if and only if it cannot be derived by valid syllogistic inference from true and prior premisses.[20]

---

[20] According to Jonathan Barnes (*Aristotle's Posterior Analytics*, pp. 156, 99), *Xba* is atomic if and only if there is no middle term *c* such that '*Yca*, *Zbc* so *Xba*' is a syllogism (*X*=*A* or *X*=*E*, *Y*=*A* or *Y*=*E*, *Z*=*A* or *Z*=*E*). (I will follow Barnes and ignore the second figure.) This analysis is inadequate; for one can construct a syllogism of *Xba* from false premisses. The natural strengthening – to require that the premisses be true – is sufficient only if one assumes that predicates form chains. Otherwise given atomic

If one knows that Xba ($X=A$ or $X=E$) is atomic, then one knows that no deduction of Yba ($Y=A$ or $Y=E$) can be a proof. If $X=Y$ the deduction cannot be revealing either the explanation of the conclusion or why the conclusion cannot be otherwise. If $X \neq Y$, then to believe the conclusion is to be led into error by deduction. So if one knows that Xba is atomic, one knows that any deduction of Yba can only be misleading.

In the light of the loss of a middle term at every syllogistic inference, Aristotle's division of his task into two – in A16 dealing with atomic and in A17 with non-atomic statements – has a clear *raison d'être*. With atomic statements it matters far less what the middle term was: simply that there was a middle term (that is, a deduction) is a criterion for error. With non-atomic statements, by contrast, some deduction may be a proof and so the concern with the information lost in the deduction will be much greater. Moreover, the knowledge that the conclusion of a deduction or its contrary is atomic enables one to recover additional information about the nature of the deduction itself; and thus partially to compensate for the loss of information in syllogistic deductions.

As I mentioned in Chapter 2, Aristotle conceived of predicates forming chains such that the predicates $b_0 b_1 \ldots b_n$ form a *chain* if each holds universally of its predecessor. Thus Aba will be atomic if b, a are contiguous in a common chain. If b and a are separated, then Aba could be derived by a, perhaps extended, derivation in *Barbara* with the predicates separating b and a functioning as middle terms.

> 'If neither is in a whole and a does not belong to b, it is necessary that it does not belong atomically. For if there is some middle term, it is necessary for one of them to be in some whole.' (*An. Pst.* A15, 79b12–15)

Any deduction of Eba has one universal affirmative premiss which asserts that either the minor term b (*Celarent, Cesare*) or the major term a (*Camestres*) is contained in the middle term. Thus it is sufficient for Eba to be atomic that b not belong to a and that neither is the subject of predication.

In *Posterior Analytics* A16 (79b29–80a5) Aristotle envisages the

---

Xba one may be able to find a middle term c with the same extension as the extremes, forming a syllogism from true premisses in *Barbara*. If one insists that there be no true and prior premisses from which Xba may be derived, the formula Xba will be atomic if and only if the predicates a and b are contiguous in a chain of predication.

following situation: Eba is atomic and one has deduced in $Barbara$
$$\frac{Abc \quad Aca.}{Aba}$$ Obviously at least one of the premises must be false. The
question is whether, knowing Eba to be atomic, one can narrow the
field of falsity. Aristotle argues that from Eba being atomic it follows
that the minor premiss Abc must be false. So that while either both
premises may be false (79b29–40) or only one premiss may be false
(79b40–80a5), if only one premiss is false, it must be Abc. 'For it is
impossible for b to be in some whole (for a was said not to belong
primitively)' (79b37ff). If Abc were true, then Aca would have to be
false. Since Aristotle restricts himself to universal statements,[21] this
implies that Eca is true. But then one could prove, by an instance of
$Celarent$, $\dfrac{Eca \quad Abc}{Eba}$ which would be witness to Eba being non-atomic.

The task of *Posterior Analytics* A17 is the study of derivations of false
conclusions, the contraries of which are provable. A sentence Aba or
Eba is non-atomic if and only if it can be derived by valid syllogistic
inference from true and prior premises. With atomic statements one
can safely ignore the question of the identity of the middle term:
simply that there was a middle term is sufficient to guarantee error. For
a true non-atomic statement, by contrast, there is some middle term
through which it can be proved. The loss of a middle term at each
syllogistic inference thus assumes increased importance. One can no
longer ignore the identity of the middle term through which the false
conclusion was erroneously derived.

The concept of appropriateness is invoked for non-atomic statements
to restore information that the syllogistic sacrifices and to aid in the
restriction of the field of falsity. A middle term c is *appropriate* with
respect to a statement Xba ($X{=}A$ or $X{=}E$) if there is a deduction of
Yba ($Y{=}A$ or $Y{=}E$) from true premises with c as the middle term[22]
(*An. Pst.* 80b20ff). Since it is not necessary that $X{=}Y$, it is possible to
have a deduction of a false conclusion through an appropriate middle
term.

If one has deduced a false conclusion through a middle term known
to be appropriate, Aristotle shows that one is able to restrict sharply the
field of falsity. For example, consider his treatment of the first figure.

---

[21] Cf. Barnes, *Aristotle's Posterior Analytics*, pp. 157–8; 164–5.
[22] Aristotle actually distinguishes what might be regarded as two different types of
appropriateness. Compare e.g. *An. Pst.* 80b20–26 with 80b26–32. Logically the distinction is not important and I shall ignore it.

Suppose one has deduced in *Celarent* $\dfrac{Eca \quad Abc}{Eba}$ a conclusion known to be

false, through an appropriate middle term. Then $\dfrac{Aca \quad Abc}{Aba}$ must be a

deduction from true premisses of non-atomic *Aba* through the appropriate middle. The appropriateness of the middle term *c* forces the minor premiss in *Celarent, Abc,* to be true. For it must also function in the deduction from true premisses of *Aba*. The major premiss of *Celarent, Eca,* must be false. If the deduction is not through an appropriate middle term, then one cannot restrict the field of falsity (*An. Pst.* 80b32–81a4).

Similarly if *Eba* and one has deduced $\dfrac{Aca \quad Abc}{Aba}$ through an appro-

priate middle, only the major premiss, *Aca,* can be – and therefore must be – false, since the minor premiss *Abc* must function in a deduction

from true premisses in *Celarent* $\dfrac{Eca \quad Abc}{Eba}$ (*An. Pst.* 81a16–20). If the

middle term is not appropriate, one can again not restrict the field of falsity.

The results of *Posterior Analytics* A16 and A17 are not dramatic. The notions of atomic belonging or not belonging and of deductions of a false conclusion through an appropriate middle term are of limited help in searching for false premisses. Nevertheless, these chapters contain hints of a philosophically fruitful logical technique. The syntactic rules of the syllogistic can be used in a search for falsity as well as in the pursuit of truth. These rules can be used not merely in moving from principles to a conclusion, but also for determining, within certain bounds, what any proof of a given conclusion must be like. The significance of these chapters lies not in successful results, but in the method employed.

6

Proof by refutation

Aristotle thought that 'principles' were non-demonstrable, and were to be apprehended by mental insight.[1] But there was a problem with the non-demonstrability thesis which even Aristotle had to face: there was disagreement about what the principles were. Heraclitus seemed to deny as basic a principle as the law of non-contradiction (*Met. Γ3*, 1005b25). Heraclitus' theories were an embarrassment to Aristotle's logical programme. On the one hand, Aristotle is prevented by his own doctrine from providing a direct proof of the law of non-contradiction. On the other hand, he is confronted with the disconcerting fact that not all people simply grasp basic principles; some go so far as to deny that they are true. In *Metaphysics Γ3,4* Aristotle sets out to resolve this dilemma, and his discussion provides insight into the nature of a justification of a basic logical law. The problem of justification is still with us. For it appears, at least initially, that if the law of non-contradiction is true, then there could be nothing more basic by means of which justification could be provided. Any purported justification would stand in at least as much need of justification as the law of non-contradiction itself.

In *Metaphysics Γ3* Aristotle makes the brave and seemingly reckless move of denying that anyone can believe the law of non-contradiction false. He states two conditions which are sufficient to ensure that a principle P is the 'firmest of all'. First, it must not be possible to be in error with respect to P (*Met. Γ3*, 1005b12). Second, P must be such that anyone who understands anything understands P (*Met. Γ3*, 1005b16). The law of non-contradiction is supposed to satisfy these conditions:

'For the same thing to belong and not to belong to the same thing and in the same respect is impossible (given any further specifications which might be added against the dialectical difficulties). This then is the firmest of all principles, for it fits the specification stated. For it is impossible for anyone to believe that the same thing is and is not, as some consider Heraclitus said – for it is not necessary that the

---

[1] Cf. *An. Pst.* B19; Barnes, *Aristotle's Posterior Analytics*, pp. 248–60; J. H. Lesher, 'The meaning of *ΝΟΥ̂Σ* in the *Posterior Analytics*'.

things one says one should also believe. But if it is not possible for contraries to belong to the same thing simultaneously (given that we add the customary specifications to this proposition too) and the opinion contrary to an opinion is that of the contradictory, then obviously it is impossible for the same person to believe simultaneously that the same thing is and is not; for anyone who made that error would be holding contrary opinions simultaneously. That is why all those who prove go back to this opinion in the end: it is in the nature of things the principle of all other axioms also.' (*Met. Γ3*, 1005b19–34)

The law that Aristotle wishes to defend is:

(LNC) $(F)(x)\neg(Fx \;\&\; \neg Fx)$.[2]

The argument is not designed to prove the law of non-contradiction, but to prove that it is impossible to disbelieve the law of non-contradiction. While there may be people, e.g. Heraclitus, who sincerely assert that the law of non-contradiction is false, Aristotle denies they can believe that. This argument sets the stage for the rest of *Metaphysics Γ3–4*. The strategy is not to try to persuade someone who does not believe the law of non-contradiction to change his mind: there is no such person to whom the attempt should be addressed.

Unfortunately this argument is problematic. Kirwan accuses Aristotle of not indicating clearly whether the argument is supposed to rule out the possibility of believing 'veiled contradictions', e.g. 'Menelaus was the king of Sparta but not of Lacedaemon.'[3] However, Kirwan's criticism is unfair. For the argument is clearly intended only to rule out the possibility of self-conscious belief in two statements known to be contradictories. If it is discovered that Gx entails $\neg Fx$ then it becomes, according to Aristotle's argument, impossible to believe that Fx and Gx. But before such a discovery there is nothing in the argument designed to exclude such a conjunction of beliefs. Aristotle is not concerned to disallow the possibility of deep, un-revealed confusions. The argument is designed to refute Heraclitus' alleged thesis which presupposed that one could believe a contradiction recognized to be such.

---

[2] As Geach points out, Aristotle did not explicitly distinguish between propositional truth and the truth of predications. Since a statement, for Aristotle, was of subject–predicate form, there would be no pressing need to distinguish between propositional and predicate negation. Neither did Aristotle distinguish between the reference of a name and what a predicate applies to. See Geach, 'Aristotle on conjunctive propositions' and 'Nominalism', in *Logic Matters*, pp. 13–27, 289–91.

[3] Christopher Kirwan, *Aristotle's Metaphysics, Books Γ, Δ, E*, pp. 89–90.

A second and more serious objection is that Aristotle's argument itself seems to depend on the law of non-contradiction. Aristotle assumes that it is not possible for contraries to apply to objects simultaneously and this, of course, need not be the case if the law of non-contradiction failed.[4] Consider the following objection: Aristotle's argument begs the question for it assumes the law of non-contradiction. Aristotle's argument is supposed to show that we must believe the law of non-contradiction. But the argument assumes that the law of non-contradiction is a law of logic and this is precisely what those who claim not to believe the law of non-contradiction deny. If we recognize of two beliefs that one is a belief that Fx and the other is a belief that $\neg Fx$, then, given that we accept the law of non-contradiction, our believing that Fx will, of course, serve as a decisive objection to our believing that $\neg Fx$ (or conversely). But is not this to beg the question? For it is only because we already believe LNC that we are willing to give up one of two contradictory beliefs when we recognize them to be contradictory.

There is a dangerous ambiguity in the claim that Aristotle's argument *assumes* the law of non-contradiction. If what is meant is that the law of non-contradiction is needed as a premiss in the argument in order to secure its validity, then the claim is false. The inference from Fx to not $\neg Fx$ is valid as it stands. To someone who objects that we beg the question by assuming the law of non-contradiction, we should respond as Achilles should have responded to the Tortoise: the inference is valid as it is and does not need supplementation with a premiss that purportedly licenses the inference.[5] We do not reject $\neg Fx$ because we have both accepted Fx *and* adopted the law of non-contradiction as

---

[4] Of course, the crucial premiss, that 'the opinion contrary to an opinion is that of the contradictory' is not substantiated by any argument and appears in itself to be extremely dubious. Barnes has provided a defence of this suspect premiss through an investigation of the conceptual relations of belief and disbelief ('The law of contradiction'). However, Barnes' *reductio* strategy depends on directly deriving a conclusion whose contradictory is alleged to be an instance of the law of non-contradiction. Such an argument is persuasive only if the law of non-contradiction is not itself in question. Further, the justification and value of the premisses in his argument depend on the law of non-contradiction. For example, in defence of premiss (1), '(x) (x Believes $(P\&Q) \supset x$ Believes P and x Believes Q)', Barnes argues that it is absurd to suppose that a man believes $P\&Q$ and does not believe Q. For, Barnes asks rhetorically, if a man does not believe Q, how could he believe P *and* Q? The situation is absurd, but the absurdity derives from the fact that we take the supposition that a man may both believe Q and not believe Q to be absurd.

[5] James Thomson, 'What the Tortoise should have said to Achilles'; Wittgenstein, *Remarks on the Foundations of Mathematics*, 1, §§6–8. Here again, I am indebted to Kripke for various discussions about these arguments.

a law of logic: we reject $\neg Fx$ simply because we have accepted Fx. It is not that having adopted non-contradiction as a law of logic one will treat acceptance of Fx as decisive grounds for rejection of $\neg Fx$. Rather it is because one does count acceptance of Fx as ruling decisively against $\neg Fx$ that one can reflect on one's practice and form an abstract principle to describe it, in this case the law of non-contradiction.

If a question-begging argument is one that tries to prove a (non-self-evident) statement by means of itself, then this argument radically fails to be question-begging in that the law of non-contradiction occurs neither as a premiss nor as conclusion. For as we have seen, Aristotle's argument is not designed to prove the law, but to prove that it is impossible to disbelieve the law of non-contradiction. Aristotle's argument that it is impossible to disbelieve the law of non-contradiction depends on the law to this extent: if the law were not true then the argument would lose all its force. Aristotle readily acknowledges this dependence.

'But we have just accepted that it is impossible to be and not be simultaneously and we have shown by means of this that it is the firmest of all principles.' (*Met. Γ*4, 1006a33ff)

To admit that the argument works *by means of* the law of non-contradiction is not to admit, as Kirwan believes,[6] that the argument depends upon LNC as a premiss. Rather it is to admit just what Aristotle believes: that our proof procedures must conform to the law of non-contradiction. In particular, the strength of the argument that it is impossible to disbelieve the law depends upon its truth. To show that the law of non-contradiction is the firmest of principles of course requires its truth: were it not true, the law could hardly be the firmest of principles.

This response indicates why Aristotle treated the laws of non-contradiction and excluded middle as 'common principles'. These laws are common because they are not premisses of argument at all, but rather principles of reason which abstractly codify aspects of our deductive inferential practice. Aristotle is clearly aware of this distinction. In *Posterior Analytics* A11 Aristotle asserts that the only proofs in which the law of non-contradiction occurs as a premiss are proofs whose conclusions are themselves instances of the law of non-contradiction (*An. Pst.* 77a10–22).[7] Aristotle seems to argue that given a

[6] Kirwan, *Aristotle's Metaphysics, Books Γ, Δ, E*, p. 90.
[7] Cf. Barnes, *Aristotle's Posterior Analytics*, p. 140.

proof with an instance of the law as conclusion, one can proof-theoretically determine that one of the premisses must be an instance of the law. Similarly, Aristotle limits the use of the law of excluded middle to *per impossibile* proofs (*An. Pst.* 77a22–27). As we saw in Chapter 3, the law of excluded middle does not occur as a premiss in a *per impossibile* proof. Rather, one directly deduces a conclusion known to be impossible from two premisses one of which is known to be true, and then simply infers the contradictory of the premiss not known to be true. In fact, Aristotle would not have been able to claim that a direct and a *per impossibile* proof yield the same conclusion from the same premisses if the law of excluded middle occurred as a premiss in the *per impossibile* proof.

Frege's formalization of logic as an axiomatized system with a minimum number of rules of inference and a relatively large number of axioms, taken to be logical truths, has deeply coloured the vision of logic held by philosophers and logicians in this century.[8] Twentieth-century interpreters of Aristotelian logic are not out of Frege's shadow – an extreme example is Łukasiewicz's formalization of the syllogistic as an axiomatic system – and the temptation to assimilate all common principles to Fregean logical truths must be resisted. One can accept that the laws of excluded middle and non-contradiction are common principles without having to accept that they occur as premisses anywhere in a proof.[9]

Still, the problems of providing a justification of as basic a logical principle as the law of non-contradiction are far from resolved. If Aristotle's argument is correct, there are no people who do not believe the law of non-contradiction, yet there may be people who sincerely *think* they do not believe it. And though they may not, strictly speaking, be able to charge Aristotle with begging the question, neither would they, when confronted with Aristotle's argument, feel any compulsion to abandon their position. For they may readily admit that *if* the law is true, then it is the firmest of principles and they must be incapable of disbelieving it. Yet what they deny is that LNC is true, and

[8] For a critique of this type of formalization, see Dummett, *Frege: Philosophy of Language,* pp. 432–41.

[9] Of course, some common principles should be treated as premisses. In *Posterior Analytics* A10–11, Aristotle mentions as a third example of a common principle the Euclidean common notion that equals taken from equals leave equals (*An. Pst.* 76a41, 77a31). Such a common principle is used as an axiom schema instances of which do occur as premisses in proofs. Thus Aristotle says that the Euclidean principle may occur in geometrical proofs as a premiss about equal lengths and in arithmetical proofs as a premiss about equal numbers.

they may take their own *alleged* belief in its negation as evidence that
the law of non-contradiction could not be the firmest of principles.

Aristotle argues that a response must take some form other than
direct proof.

'Some, owing to lack of training, actually demand that it [LNC] be
proved: for it is lack of training not to recognize of which things
proof ought to be sought and of which not. For in general it is
impossible that there should be proof of everything, since it would
go on to infinity so that not even thus would it be proof. But if there
are some things of which proof ought not to be sought, they could
not say what they regard as a principle more fully of that kind. But
even this can be proved to be impossible in the manner of a refutation
if only the disputant says something. If he says nothing, it is ridicu-
lous to look for a statement in response to one who has a statement of
nothing, in so far as he has not; such a person, in so far as he is such,
is similar to a vegetable. By 'proving in the manner of a refutation' I
mean something different from proving, because in proving one
might be thought to beg the original [question], but if someone else
is cause of such a thing it must be refutation and not proof. In
response to every case of that kind the original [step] is not to ask
him to state something either to be or not to be (for that might well
be believed to beg what was originally at issue), but at least to
signify something both to himself and to someone else; for that is
necessary if he is to say anything.' (*Met.* Γ4, 1006a5–22)

Proof has its limitations. By its very nature, a proof enables one to gain
knowledge of the conclusion based upon a knowledge of the premisses.
But the problem is not to prove the law of non-contradiction from
prior principles but to *respond* to someone who seems to be denying it.
Attempting to show the incoherence of his position in the most direct
manner possible, we may initially have said 'Given that you accept *Fa*,
then it is not the case that not *Fa*, therefore it is not the case that (*Fa*
and not *Fa*).' Our opponent charges us with begging the question,
since the validity of our inference depends upon the law of non-contradiction being valid. We may not be able to offer a direct proof of the
law of non-contradiction which will not be seen to beg the question.

Proof by 'refutation' is Aristotle's response to someone who charges
us with begging the question in our attempt to justify the law of non-
contradiction. We are not in a position to return the compliment: we
cannot charge our disputant with question-begging, for he is not trying

to prove the negation of the law of non-contradiction by means of itself. What Aristotle does charge him with, however, is a covert dependence on the law of non-contradiction. Proof by refutation is designed to show that the possibility of *saying anything*, even that the law of non-contradiction is false, depends on an adherence to the law of non-contradiction. If a person is to deny the law of non-contradiction he must be in a position to do just that: assert that the law is false. There is no point, says Aristotle, in trying to argue with someone who says nothing; for in so far as he says nothing he is no better than a vegetable (*Met. Γ*4, 1006a15). But Aristotle is not arguing with a vegetable. He is arguing with someone who can present a coherent, if fallacious, argument for the falsity of the law of non-contradiction. The opponent of the law, while disowning reason, listens to reason (*Met. Γ*4, 1006a26). He is able to argue in a reasoned way against the law of non-contradiction and the possibility of such argumentation depends on adherence to the law of non-contradiction.

If someone is *to say anything* – even that the law of non-contradiction is false – he must 'signify something' both to himself and to others (*Met. Γ*4, 1006a21–22). Aristotle's strategy is to show that the possibility of signifying something depends upon adherence to the law of non-contradiction. To understand the argument, an excursion into the realm of Aristotelian semantics is necessary. A sentence, for Aristotle, is a significant spoken sound, made up of expressions that themselves signify.[10] Statements, those sentences capable of truth or falsity, are divided into affirmations and negations (*De Int.* 16b33, 17a8). An affirmation is a statement affirming something of something and a negation is a statement denying something of something (*De Int.* 17a25ff). These, for Aristotle, are the paradigms of a sentence: that a predicate does or does not apply to a subject.

Since in an Aristotelian statement one either affirms or denies something of a subject, at least part of the semantic role of the subject-term must be to pick out, refer to, the subject about which the affirmation or denial is being made. For an affirmation could affirm something *of* something only if the subject-term picked out the subject of which something is being affirmed. I would like to suggest that what an expression signifies corresponds to its semantic role: it follows that at

---

[10] *De Int.* 16b26. Names and verbs, the components of sentences both signify. *De Int.* 16a19–21, 16b6, 16b19. See also *Categories* 1b25: the 'things said without combination' are the semantically significant subsentential units, '. . . each signifies either a substance or quantity or a relative or having or doing or being affected'.

least part of what it is for a subject-term to signify is for it to refer to the substance about which a predication is being made.[11] Aristotle makes this point (though imprecisely, owing to a failure to distinguish use and mention):

'Every substance seems to signify a certain 'this'. As regards primary substance it is indisputably true that each of them signifies a certain this; for the thing revealed is atomic and numerically one.' (*Cat.* 3b10–13)

A name of a primary substance, for example, 'Socrates' signifies the particular Socrates who, being a 'this', is individual and numerically one. Concerning natural kind terms (that is, names for secondary substances) Aristotle is more cautious (*Cat.* 3b13–21). The problem is to avoid reference to objects like Platonic Forms. Thus 'man' does not actually signify a certain 'this', even though it may appear to do so. For *man* is not an individual, as a primary substance is, but is *said of* many things.[12] However, unlike e.g. 'white', which only signifies a certain qualification, natural kind terms *signify substance* of a certain qualification (*Cat.* 3b20–21). Natural kind terms such as 'man' signify, at least in part, by referring to individual men.[13] This theme is pursued in the theory of predication developed in *Posterior Analytics* A22. Metaphysically misleading sentences, e.g. 'The white thing is a man', are dismissed as either not predicating at all or as predicating only incidentally (*An. Pst.* 83a14–32). In genuine predications one thing is predicated of a subject and one is saying either what the subject is – e.g. 'man is animal' – or saying that the subject has some property – e.g. 'man is white' (*An. Pst.* 83a21–23). Aristotle continues:

> 'Again, the things signifying a substance signify of what they are predicated of just what is that thing or just what is a particular sort of it; but the things which do not signify a substance but are said of some other underlying subject which is neither just what is that thing nor just what is a particular sort of it, are incidental, e.g. white of the man. For the man is neither just what is white nor just what is some white – but presumably animal; for a man is just what is an animal. But the things which do not signify a substance must be predicated of some underlying subject and there cannot be anything white which is not white through being something different. (For we can say goodbye to the Forms; for they are nonsense, and if they exist they are nothing to the argument; for proofs are about things of this type.)' (*An. Pst.* 83a24–35)

To signify a substance is not only to refer to a particular substance, but also to invoke its essence. 'Man' is not only predicated of an individual man, but it picks him out *qua* what he is. 'The white thing' may refer to a man, but it does not pick him out *qua* what he is: 'For the man is not just what is white nor just what is a certain white' (*An. Pst.* 83a29). Substance-terms, by contrast, signify just what that thing is of which they are predicated (*An. Pst.* 83a24).[14]

If a man is to say anything, he must signify something both to himself and to someone else. 'For if he does not there would be no statement for such a person either in response to himself or to anyone else' (*Met.* Γ4, 1006a21–24). Any statement must affirm or deny something of something; and the subject term must signify the substance of which the affirmation or denial is made.[15]

[14] The connection would be even easier to forge if an individual substance were its essence. For a defence of this thesis, see Hartman, 'Aristotle on the identity of substance and essence'. But on the other side see Albritton, 'Forms of particular substances in Aristotle's *Metaphysics*'. Cf. also *An. Pst.* Δ4, 73b5–10.

[15] That is why Aristotle's claim that the phrase 'goat stag' signifies is not damaging to this interpretation. Aristotle says that the name 'goat stag' signifies but, because there are none, it is impossible to know what a goat stag is (*An. Pst.* Β7 92b4–8). Remember, to say that an expression signifies is only to say that it has a semantic role. One can allow that the term 'goat stag' has a semantic role, that it signifies, without maintaining it must refer to goat stags. It would only refer to goat stags if it were a genuine substance-

'... it is clear then that this at least is itself true, that the name signifies to be or not to be this particular thing, so that it could not be that everything was thus and not thus. Again if man signifies one thing, let that be biped animal. What I mean by signifying one thing is this: if this is a man, then if anything is a man that thing will be to be a man.' (*Met. Γ*4, 1006a28–34)

If the name signifies one thing, it will do more than merely refer to an individual or individuals. If 'man' signifies one thing then any individual man will be what it is to be a man.

This interpretation is supported by Aristotle's distinction between 'signifying' one thing and 'signifying about' one thing:

'Then it is not possible that "to be a man" signifies just what "not to be a man" [signifies], if "man" signifies not only about one thing but also one thing (for we do not count as signifying one thing this, viz. signifying about one thing, since in that way "musical" and "white" and "man" would signify one thing, so that all will be one, because synonymous). And it will not be to be and not to be the same thing unless homonymously, as if others were to call not-man what we call man. But what is puzzling is not whether it is possible that the same thing should simultaneously be and not be a man in name, but in fact.' (*Met. Γ*4, 1006b13–22)

'Signify about' can be interpreted as 'be truly predicated of'.[16] Aristotle's point is that even if 'man', 'white' and 'musical' could be truly predicated of some pallid lyre-player, the terms would not all signify one and the same thing. Only 'man' is a subject-term and signifies a substance, an individual man; what it is for this substance to be is to be a man. Being white or musical are properties of an individual subject, but they are properties the subject can gain or lose while remaining that subject. It is characteristic of a subject that it can undergo such change. But there are some changes a subject cannot undergo and remain that subject: a subject cannot at one time be a man and later

---

16 Cf. Kirwan, *Aristotle's Metaphysics, Books Γ, Δ, E*, p. 96.

term; for then its semantic role would be, at least in part, to refer to the subjects of a predication. Aristotle need not deny that 'goat stag' signifies. He is only committed to the fact that 'goat stag' cannot be the subject-term of a statement – a sentence capable of truth or falsity. For a statement affirms or denies something of something and there are no such things as goat stags of which to affirm or deny anything.

fail to be a man. For if he is a man, then that is just what it is for him to be.[17]

Aristotle says that if 'man' and 'musical' and 'white' signified one thing 'all will be one because synonymous' (*Met.* Γ4 1006b17–18). Here, one must not interpret 'synonymous' in terms of the modern concept of synonymity and mistakenly infer that what a term signifies is a statement of its meaning. For Aristotle it is not words but things which are synonymous. Two things are synonymous if they share not only a name in common, but also the 'definition of being' that corresponds to the name (*Cat.* 1a7).[18] Here the 'definition of being' need not be thought of as merely verbal:[19] to state that biped animal is the definition of man is not to say that the linguistic expression 'man' means 'biped animal'; rather it is to say that to be a biped animal is what it is to be a man. Similarly, if biped animal is what 'man' signifies, it is not that 'biped animal' gives the verbal definition of what 'man' means.[20] If 'man', 'white' and 'musical' signified one thing, then man, white and musical would share definition of being: an individual man would be just what it is to be musical and white. Aristotle says that all will be one because synonymous: this means that if things share not merely a name but the definition that corresponds to the name, then they are essentially the same thing.[21]

---

[17] Noonan has suggested that two predicates F and G have the same signification if and only if $\Box(x) (Fx \leftrightarrow Gx)$ ('Aristotle on the principle of non-contradiction'). He then uses this analysis to contrast it with predicates signifying about one thing – i.e. predicates with the same extension. An interpretation of 1006b15ff follows. The problem with Noonan's interpretation is that while his analysis attributes a valid argument to Aristotle, it imports too much strength into the notion of signifying to achieve this end. It is not that the signification of a term is its necessary extension, but that a subject-term like 'man' signifies a substance which, while it exists, must be a man. It is the notion of substance, not signifying, which enables Aristotle to make the distinction between signifying one thing and signifying about one thing.

[18] Two objects may be both homonymous and synonymous: if a name and corresponding definition applies to both objects, and a different name applies to both objects, but there is no unique corresponding definition which also does. See Ackrill, *Aristotle's Categories and De Interpretatione*, p. 71.

[19] See Ackrill, *Aristotle's Categories and De Interpretatione*, pp. 71–91; Hamlyn, 'Aristotle on predication'.

[20] For a very different interpretation, see Dancy, *Sense and Contradiction: A Study in Aristotle* (especially p. 46). Dancy takes what a word signifies to be its sense and is thus led to make criticisms of Aristotle that I do not think are justified.

[21] Aristotle says on a number of occasions that if contradictory predicates are true of the same thing, then everything will be one. (Cf. e.g. 1006b17, 1007a6, 1007b20.) A common interpretation of Aristotle's argument attributes to him a tacit and unjustified assumption that his opponent believes the law of non-contradiction fails quite generally. It also attributes to Aristotle a belief in the identity of indiscernibles (cf. e.g. Dancy,

'It is therefore necessary if it is true of anything to say that it is a man, that it be a biped animal (for that was what "man" signified) and if that is necessary it is not possible that the same thing should not be, at the same time, a biped animal (for to be necessary signifies this: to be impossible not to be). Therefore it is not possible that it should be simultaneously true to say that the same thing is a man and is not a man.' (*Met. Γ*4, 1006b28–34)

'Man' signifies biped animal; so we can say of anything that is a man that it is a biped animal (cf. *Cat.* 2a19). The necessity derives from the fact that 'man' signifies a substance, an individual man. What it is for him to be is to be a biped animal: so it is not possible that *he* should not be a biped animal. For if he is anything he is that. But if we cannot say of him that he is not a biped animal, we cannot say of him that he is not a man, for not-man and not-biped-animal are said of the same things.[22]

This argument is persuasive only if one accepts Aristotle's view of substance. One must accept that there are, for example, individual men and that there is something which is just what it is to be a man; for example, a biped animal. For then it makes no sense to say that *it* is not a biped animal: if it is anything at all it must be a biped animal. Someone who did not believe in substance, however, need not be persuaded. Contrapositively, Aristotle accuses those who deny LNC of destroying substance:

'Those who say this entirely destroy substance and what it is to be. For it is necessary for them to maintain that all things are coincidences and there is no such thing as just what to be a man or to be an

---

[22] Cf. *De Int.* 16a29; Ackrill, *Aristotle's Categories and De Interpretatione*, pp. 117–18.

Sense and Contradiction: A Study in Aristotle, p. 47). Since both F and $\neg F$ are supposed to apply to all x, it follows from the identity of indiscernibles that everything will be one.

There is however an alternative interpretation, based on the notion of signifying a substance, that permits an explanation of why Aristotle thought his opponent committed to the universal failure of the law of non-contradiction. Further the interpretation does not require attributing to Aristotle a belief in the identity of indiscernibles. By the law of excluded middle, (x) (man(x) v not-man(x)). 'Not-man' will be true of everything in the universe that is not a man. Suppose now that 'man' and 'not-man' signify one thing. Then since part of what it is for a subject-term to signify is to 'refer' to those objects of which it is true, it follows that (x) (man(x) & not-man(x)). Further since the terms 'man' and 'not-man' signify one thing, then those things signified are signified in virtue of their being what they are. However, everything is signified by these terms. The universe will thus be essentially homogeneous.

animal [is]. For if anything is just what to be a man [is], that will not be to be a not-man or not to be a man: yet those are its denials. For what it signified was one thing and that was something's substance and to signify a thing's substance is to signify that being, for it, is nothing else.' (*Met. Γ*4, 1007a20–27)

If 'not-man' could be said of the very same individual of which 'man' is said, there could not be substance, for there would be nothing which is just what a man is. Then the possibility of discourse is destroyed for there is no subject about which to make any affirmation or denial:

'For if everything is said incidentally there will not be anything which things are initially about if coincidental always signifies a predication about a certain subject.' (*Met. Γ*4, 1007a33–b1)

But coincidental properties do coincide in a subject. The white may be musical and the musical white, but that is because they both coincide in an individual man; e.g. the talented but pallid musician (*Met. Γ*4, 1007b2–17). If coincidental properties always coincide in a subject, then any account that destroys substance must be incorrect.

'Consequently, there will be something signifying a substance even in such a case. And if that is so, it has been shown that it is impossible to predicate contradictories simultaneously.' (*Met. Γ*4, 1007b16–18)

A true opponent of the law of non-contradiction is robbed of the possibility of saying anything. For to say something, on the Aristotelian semantics, is to predicate a property of a subject. And if we attempt to say of a subject both that it is man and that it is not-man we have not succeeded in making two predications; we have failed to make one.

A serious objection to Aristotle's argument is that it assumes a particular semantical picture. A statement is assumed to be of the subject–predicate form and an affirmation is true if the predicate applies to the subject and false otherwise. The world is like a classical model of subjects and properties; it is a model that embodies the laws of classical logic. Given such a semantical picture, it does not make sense to say that a property does and does not hold of a subject. But why should a sophisticated opponent of LNC accept such a semantics? Consider, for example, Aristotle's defence of the law of excluded middle in *Metaphysics Γ*7. 'There is,' says Aristotle, 'no alteration except into opposites.' Were there a middle between 'white' and 'not-white' there would be a process of coming-to-be-white from something other than not-

white and this, says Aristotle, is not observed (*Met. Γ*7, 1011b34ff). He
argues that the negation of a statement 'not-white (*x*)' is compatible
with every state of affairs other than *x* being white. And since 'white
(*x*)' holds in the one situation in which its negation does not, Aristotle
argues that 'white (*x*) or not-white (*x*)' must be valid (*Met. Γ*7,
1012a15ff).

An opponent may, however, respond by rejecting the semantics, by
denying that 'white' is a determinate predicate which either applies or
fails to apply to every object. 'White', it may be objected, is a vague
predicate: for certain objects in the domain of discourse, there may be
no determinate answer as to whether they satisfy 'white' or 'not-white'.
Crispin Wright has proposed the following Sorites paradox:[23] there is
a series of colour patches, the first patch being obviously white and
each patch visually indistinguishable from its immediate successor. Yet
the last patch in the series is very dark; that is, obviously not white.
Now if the opponent can convince us that 'white' is an observational
predicate – that is, one for which the criteria of application are based
solely on our perceptual powers – and if, as in the imagined case, there
is a failure of transitivity in the relation '... is visually indistinguishable
from ...' then it seems one must at least countenance the possibility
that there may be cases for which there is no determinate answer as to
which predicate, 'white' or 'not-white', applies.[24] The opponent's
objection is at least *prima facie* cogent because Aristotle's semantics
does not allow for the possibility of vagueness.

In the case of the law of non-contradiction, a sophisticated opponent
may make an objection to Aristotelian semantics so radical that we do
not find it even *prima facie* compelling. Nevertheless, it seems as if
Aristotle does not even *allow* for this possibility. He argues that an
opponent of LNC must eliminate substance and so there can be nothing
that his statements are about. But that an opponent cannot *say anything*
seems to follow only if one assumes that the correct semantical account
of all statements is that a predicate applies or does not apply to a subject. The very way in which Aristotle defines a contradiction and poses
an objection to the law of non-contradiction assumes an ontology of
subjects about which our language speaks. In a contradiction 'the
negation must deny *the same thing* as the affirmation affirmed and *of the
same thing* ...' (*De Int.* 17b38). Similarly, the opponent of the law of

[23] Wright, 'Language-mastery and the Sorites paradox'.
[24] I am completely ignoring the intuitionist critique of the correct semantical account of
non-atomic sentences.

non-contradiction as Aristotle thinks of him is not someone who completely gives up on an ontology of subjects and properties, but rather is someone who asserts the opposite of the law; that it *is* possible for the same thing to belong and not to belong simultaneously and in the same respect (*Met. Γ*3, 1005b23). But why could not a more sophisticated opponent reject the semantics completely? Could he not hold that, since the law of non-contradiction is false, Aristotle's argument only shows that we must give up the picture of the world as composed of subjects and properties? The truth of sentences would then have to be accounted for in ways that did not invoke the existence of substance.

The response to this objection is that in Aristotle's proof by refutation a valid point is being made which transcends the semantical context in which it occurs. An assertion divides up the world: to assert that anything is the case one must exclude other possibilities. This exclusion is just what fails to occur in the absence of the law of non-contradiction, even when construed in its most general propositional form: $\neg (P \ \& \ \neg P)$. One cannot assert P and then directly proceed to assert $\neg P$: one does not succeed in making a second assertion, but only in cancelling the first assertion. This is the ultimate reason why an opponent of the law of non-contradiction cannot say anything.

'... it follows that everyone would have the truth and everyone would be in error and [the disputant] acknowledges himself to be in error. At the same time it is evident that in response to this person there is nothing for an investigation to deal with; for he says nothing. For he says neither that it is thus, nor that it is not thus, but that it is both thus and not thus; and again he also denies both these, saying that it is neither thus nor not thus.' (*Met. Γ*4, 1008a28–33)

The opponent of the law of non-contradiction (if he is consistent) must admit not only that what he says is true, but also that what he says is in error. This seems to be the paradigm of proof by refutation: the opponent is forced to say that what he says is false.

Why, however, should this opponent be bothered? That everything he says is false does not for him rule out the possibility that everything he says is also true, which he also firmly believes. In fact he should cheerfully admit that everything he says is false – *of course* it is false – and he should chide us for not seeing that it is false (and true) as well. (Similarly with Aristotle's argument at *Met. Γ*4, 1006b28 that it is not possible for the same thing to be a man and not be a man. Why cannot

the opponent agree that it is not possible, but also conclude that it is?)
Why should the opponent object to any inference we make? Should he
not accept all the inferences we accept as valid and complain only that
we have not recognized all the valid inferences? (Of course, he should
also say that we have recognized all the valid inferences.) Further, he
may charge us with begging the question (*Met. Γ*4, 1008b1), for the
objection only appears to be an objection if one accepts the law of non-
contradiction.

However, Aristotle's proof by refutation has a purpose more pro-
found than the mere attempt to extract a confession of error from his
opponent. Earlier it was argued that Aristotle's argument that no one
can believe a contradiction was only meant to apply to contradictions
recognized to be such; it was not designed to rule out the possibility of
holding contradictory beliefs that are not recognized to be contradictory. His argument is not primarily intended for the 'opponent' of the
law of non-contradiction, whoever he is; it is addressed to the reader
or, if you will, the back benches of the Academy. The proof by means
of refutation is constructed so as to reveal *to us* that Aristotle's opponent is in a contradictory position. *Prima facie* it might appear that the
revelation that one is in a contradictory position would hardly be felt as
damaging to the opponent of the law of non-contradiction. But
Aristotle is not trying to persuade him: the argument is for our sake,
not for his. Aristotle thinks he has shown that there is no one who does
not believe the law of non-contradiction. So the strategy to adopt is one
designed to get *us* to see the incoherent position Aristotle's opponent is
in.

This cannot be achieved merely by having him admit that he is in
error. Although he admits to this we do not yet recognize the incoherence of his position. Proof by means of refutation is designed to show
us that if the opponent is capable of saying anything – even if what he
is capable of saying is that he is opposed to the law of non-contradiction
– then his assertive and inferential practices, his general behaviour,
must be in accord with the law of non-contradiction.[25] And when a man

25 Philosophers have long argued that there can be no justification of basic deductive
inferences or basic logical laws because any attempted justification will make recourse
to the very inference or law one is trying to justify. Dummett has responded that one
must distinguish between a suasive and an explanatory argument ('The justification of
deduction'). If the task of a proof is to convince, then the epistemic direction of the
argument must be the same as the consequential direction of the proof. In virtue of
one's knowledge of the premises one becomes convinced of the truth of the conclusion.
With a proof used in an explanatory role, the epistemic direction may be the reverse of
the consequential: knowing that the conclusion is true we may construct an argument

is sufficiently confused to assert that he does not believe in the law of non-contradiction, his general behaviour is a far better guide to his beliefs than his assertions. That he will walk to Megara rather than stay where he is when he considers that he should walk there, that he will do one thing rather than another reveals decisively that he is not the opponent of the law of non-contradiction that he thinks he is (*Met. Γ4,* 1008b12–27). Were he a true opponent he would not think Aristotle's arguments damaging, but neither would he think anything else – he would be a vegetable. Even in such a case we could not justly call him a 'true opponent' of the law of non-contradiction, for we would not be able to ascribe to him any beliefs at all. Proof by means of refutation reveals that if we can ascribe any beliefs to him, if we can interpret him as saying anything, then he must believe the law of non-contradiction, whatever sincere beliefs about his beliefs he may hold to the contrary. The opponent of the law of non-contradiction tries to argue rationally that one should not accept it. Aristotle's point is that there is no conceptual space in which such a rational discussion can occur. Argumentation is useless to persuade him to 'accept the law of non-contradiction', whatever that might mean, but his very ability to argue reveals that the alleged opponent is not genuine, even though we may have thought he was. The opponent *may* cheerfully admit that everything he says is false and, momentarily, we may even find that amusing, but after the proof by refutation we will not find it deeply interesting.

---

which would shed light on why it is true. The distinction between suasive and explanatory arguments provides an escape from the charge of circularity in any attempt to justify a basic deductive inference or logical law. For the man who seeks justification does no thave to be persuaded that the inference is valid; he simply wishes to have its validity explained. Aristotle's proof by refutation brings the inadequacy of Dummett's position to light. The suasive appearance of *Metaphysics Γ3, 4* can be misleading. Aristotle's Heraclitus does not seek explanation: he thinks he understands the law perfectly well and he thinks that it is false. Yet the argument is not designed to convince him – it is designed to convince us, the reader and the back benches of the Academy. This, however, does not mean that the argument need not be suasive. For there may be those among us who find Heraclitus' argument attractive. But they are not thinking clearly: the person Aristotle must convince is not someone who does not believe the law of non-contradiction, but only someone who thinks he does not believe it. Proof by means of refutation is designed to reveal to anyone who thinks he does not believe the law of non-contradiction the incoherence of his position.

Bibliography

Ackrill, J. L., *Aristotle's Categories and De Interpretatione*, Clarendon Press, Oxford, 1963.

Albritton, R., 'Forms of particular substances in Aristotle's *Metaphysics*', *Journal of Philosophy*, 1959.

Annas, J., *Aristotle's Metaphysics M and N*, Clarendon Press, Oxford, 1976.

Anscombe, G. E. M., and Geach, P. T., *Three Philosophers*, Basil Blackwell, Oxford, 1961.

Aristotelis, *Analytica Priora Et Posteriora*, W. D. Ross (ed.), Clarendon Press, Oxford, 1968.

  Categoriae·Et Liber De Interpretatione, L. Minio Paluello (ed.), Clarendon Press, Oxford, 1974.

  Ethica Nicomachea, L. Bywater (ed.), Clarendon Press, Oxford, 1975.

  Metaphysica, W. Jaeger (ed.), Clarendon Press, Oxford, 1973.

  Physica, W. D. Ross (ed.), Clarendon Press, Oxford, 1973.

  Topica Et Sophistici Elenchi, W. D. Ross (ed.), Clarendon Press, Oxford, 1974.

Barnes, Jonathan, 'The Law of contradiction', *Philosophical Quarterly*, 1969.

  'Aristotle's Theory of Demonstration', *Phronesis*, 1969.

  Aristotle's Posterior Analytics, Clarendon Press, Oxford, 1975.

  'Aristotle, Menaechmus and circular proof', *Classical Quarterly*, 1976.

  review of Hintikka and Remes (1974): *Mind*, 1977.

  Malcolm Schofield, Richard Sorabji (eds.), *Articles on Aristotle*, 1. Science, Duckworth, 1975.

Benacerraf, Paul, 'What numbers could not be', *Philosophical Review*, 1965.

  'Mathematical truth', *The Journal of Philosophy*, 1973.

  and Putnam, Hilary (eds.), *Philosophy of Mathematics: Selected Readings*, Prentice-Hall, 1964.

Bernays, Paul, 'On Platonism in mathematics', in Benacerraf and Putnam (1964).

Bochenski, I. M., *A History of Formal Logic*, Chelsea Publishing Company, New York, 1970.

Bolton, R., 'Essentialism and semantic theory in Aristotle: *Posterior Analytics* II, 7–10', *Philosophical Review*, 1976.

Bonitz, H., *Index Aristotelicus*, W. De Gruyter, reissued 1961.

Boolos, G., 'The iterative conception of set', *The Journal of Philosophy*, 1971.

Carroll, Lewis (Charles Dodgson), *Symbolic Logic Part I, Elementary*, Macmillan, 1896.

Cherniss, H., 'Plato as a mathematician', *The Review of Metaphysics*, 1951.

  Aristotle's Criticism of Plato and the Academy, volume 1, Russell and Russell, New York, 1972.

Church, A., *Introduction to Mathematical Logic*, volume 1, Princeton University Press, 1956.

Corcoran, J., 'Completeness of an ancient logic', *The Journal of Symbolic Logic*, 1972.

'Conceptual structure of classical logic', *Philosophy and Phenomenological Research*, volume 33, 1972, State University of New York at Buffalo.

'A mathematical model of Aristotle's syllogistic', *Archiv für Geschichte der Philosophie*, 1973.

'Aristotelian syllogisms: valid arguments or true universalized conditionals?', *Mind*, 1974a.

(ed.), *Ancient Logic and Its Modern Interpretations*, D. Reidel, 1974b.

'Aristotle's natural deduction system', in J. Corcoran (1974b).

Cornford, F. M., 'Mathematics and dialectic in the Republic vi–vii', *Mind*, 1932.

Dancy, R. M., *Sense and Contradiction: A Study in Aristotle*, D. Reidel, 1975.

DeMorgan, A., *Formal Logic*, second edition, A. E. Taylor (ed.), Open Court, London, 1926.

Demos, R., 'The structure of substance according to Aristotle', *Philosophy and Phenomenological Research*, 1944/5.

Dodgson, C., 'What the Tortoise said to Achilles', *Mind*, 1895.

Dummett, Michael, *Frege: Philosophy of Language*, Duckworth, 1973.

'The philosophical basis of intuitionism', in H. E. Rose, J. C. Shepherdson (eds.), *Logic Colloquium '73, Proceedings of the Logic Colloquium, Bristol, 1973*, North Holland, 1975.

'What is a theory of meaning? ii', in Gareth Evans and John McDowell (1976).

Elements of Intuitionism, Clarendon Press, Oxford, 1977.

'Truth', *Truth and Other Enigmas*, Duckworth, 1978.

'The justification of deduction', *Truth and Other Enigmas*.

Ebbinghaus, K., 'Ein formales Modell der aristotelischen Syllogistic', *Hypomnemata* 9, Göttingen, 1965.

Evans, D. G., *Aristotle's Concept of Dialectic*, Cambridge University Press, 1977.

Evans, Gareth and McDowell, John (eds.), *Truth and Meaning: Essays in Semantics*, Clarendon Press, Oxford, 1976.

Fitch, F., *Symbolic Logic, An Introduction*, Ronald Press, New York, 1952.

Elements of Combinatory Logic, Yale University Press, 1974.

Fraenkel, A., Bar-Hillel, J., *et al. Foundations of Set Theory*, North Holland, 1973.

Frege, G., *The Foundations of Arithmetic, Die Grundlagen der Arithmetik*, Basil Blackwell, 1968.

Logical Investigations, Basil Blackwell, 1977.

Geach, P. T., *Logic Matters*, Basil Blackwell, 1972.

Reason and Argument, Basil Blackwell, 1976.

Gentzen, Gerhard, 'Investigations into logical deduction', 'The consistency of elementary number theory', in M. E. Szabo (ed.), *The Collected Papers of Gerhard Gentzen*, North Holland, 1969.

Gulley, N., 'Greek geometrical analysis', *Phronesis*, 1958.

Hacking, Ian, 'What is logic?', *The Journal of Philosophy*, 1979.

Hamblin, C. L., *Fallacies*, Methuen, 1970.

Hamlyn, D. W., 'Aristotle on predication', *Phronesis*, 1961.

Hartman, E., 'Aristotle on the identity of substance and essence', *Philosophical Review*, 1976.

Heath, T. L., *The Thirteen Books of Euclid's Elements*, Dover, 1956.
Mathematics in Aristotle, Clarendon Press, Oxford, 1970.
History of Greek Mathematics, Clarendon Press, Oxford, 1971.
Hilbert, D., 'On the infinite', Benacerraf and Putnam (1964).
'On the foundations of logic and arithmetic', in van Heijenoort (1971).
Hintikka, J., 'On the ingredients of an Aristotelian science', *NOῩΣ*, 1972.
Time and Necessity, Clarendon Press, Oxford, 1973.
and Remes, U., *The Method of Analysis*, D. Reidel, 1974.
Jaeger, W., *Aristotle: Fundamentals of the History of His Development*, Oxford University Press, 1948.
Jaśkowski, S., 'On the rules of suppositions in formal logic', in Storrs McCall (ed.), *Polish Logic, 1920–1939*, Clarendon Press, Oxford, 1967.
Jech, T., *The Axiom of Choice*, North Holland, 1973.
Keynes, J. N., *Studies and Exercises in Formal Logic*, Macmillan, 1928.
Kirwan, Christopher, *Aristotle's Metaphysics Γ,Δ,Ε*, Clarendon Press, Oxford, 1971.
Kleene, S. C., *Introduction to Metamathematics*, North Holland, 1952.
Kneale, William and Martha, *The Development of Logic*, Clarendon Press, Oxford, 1965.
Kreisel, G. 'A survey of proof theory', *The Journal of Symbolic Logic*, 1968.
'A survey of proof theory II', in J. Fenstad (ed.), *Proceedings of the Second Scandinavian Logic Symposium*, North Holland, 1971.
Kripke, Saul A., 'Naming and necessity', in D. Davidson and G. Harman (eds.), *Semantics of Natural Language*, D. Reidel, 1972.
Lemmon, E. J., *Beginning Logic*, Nelson, 1965.
Lesher, J. H., 'The meaning of *NOῩΣ* in the *Posterior Analytics*', *Phronesis*, 1973.
Long, Peter, 'Possibility and actuality', *Mind*, 1961.
Łukasiewicz, Jan, *Aristotle's Syllogistic from the Standpoint of Modern Formal Logic*, Clarendon Press, Oxford, 1972.
Mahoney, M. S., 'Another look at Greek geometrical analysis', *Archive for History of the Exact Sciences* 5, 1968–69.
Martin, D. A., 'Sets versus classes', unpublished.
McDowell, John, 'Truth conditions, bivalence and verificationism', in Gareth Evans and John McDowell (1976).
Mendelson, E., *Introduction to Mathematical Logic*, Van Nostrand, 1964.
Mill, J. S., *A System of Logic*, Longmans Green, 1843.
Mueller, Ian, 'Aristotle on geometrical objects', *Archiv für Geschichte der Philosophie*, 1970.
'Greek mathematics and Greek logic', in J. Corcoran (1974b).
review of Hintikka and Remes (1974), *The Journal of Philosophy*, 1976.
Noonan, Harold, 'Aristotle on the principle of non-contradiction', *Analysis*, June 1977.
Owen, G. E. L., 'Logic and metaphysics in some earlier works of Aristotle', *Aristotle and Plato in the Mid Fourth Century*, I. During and G. E. L. Owen (eds.), Göteborg, 1960.
'τιθέναι τὰ φαινόμενα', in S. Mansion (ed.), *Aristote et les problèmes de méthode*, Publications Universitaires, Louvain, 1961.

'The Platonism of Aristotle', *Proceedings of the British Academy*, 1965.
(ed.), *Aristotle on Dialectic: The Topics, Proceedings of the Third Symposium Aristotelicum*, Clarendon Press, Oxford, 1968.
'Dialectic and eristic in the treatment of the Forms', in G. E. L. Owen (1968).
Patzig, G., *Aristotle's Theory of the Syllogism*, D. Reidel, 1968.
Prawitz, Dag, *Natural Deduction: A Proof-Theoretical Study*, Almquist and Wiksell, Stockholm, 1965.
'Ideas and results in proof theory', in J. Fenstad (ed.), *Proceedings of the Second Scandinavian Logic Symposium*, North Holland, 1971.
'Toward a foundation of a general proof theory', in P. Suppes, L. Henkin *et al.* (eds.), *Logic, Methodology and the Philosophy of Science IV, Proceedings of the 1971 International Congress*, North Holland, 1973.
'On the idea of a general proof theory', *Synthese*, 1974.
Putnam, Hilary, *Philosophical Papers*, volumes 1 and 2, Cambridge University Press, 1975.
Robinson, R., 'Analysis in Greek geometry', *Mind*, 1936.
Rose, Lynn E., *Aristotle's Syllogistic*, Charles Thomas, Springfield, Illinois, 1968.
Ross, W. D., *Aristotle's Prior and Posterior Analytics*, Clarendon Press, Oxford, 1965.
(ed.), *The Works of Aristotle Translated Into English*, Clarendon Press, Oxford, from 1967.
Aristotle's Metaphysics, Clarendon Press, Oxford, 1975.
Saccherio, Hieronymo, *Logica Demonstrativa, Theologicis, Philosophicis & Mathematicis Disciplinis accommodata* (third edition, Cologne), 1735.
Shoesmith, D. and Smiley, T. J., *Multiple Conclusion Logic*, Cambridge University Press, 1978.
Shorey, P., '*Συλλογισμοὶ ἐξ ὑποθέσεως* in Aristotle', *American Journal of Philology*, 1889.
Skolem, Thoraf, *Selected Works in Logic*, J. E. Fenstad (ed.), Oslo, Universitetsforlaget, 1970.
Smiley, T. J., 'Syllogism and quantification', *The Journal of Symbolic Logic*, 1962.
'What is a syllogism?', *Journal of Philosophical Logic*, 1972.
Tarski, A., *A Decision Method for Elementary Algebra and Geometry*, Berkeley, 1951.
'On the concept of logical consequence', *Logic, Semantics and Metamathematics*, Oxford University Press, 1956.
'What is elementary geometry?', in L. Henkin, P. Suppes, A. Tarski (eds.), *The Axiomatic Method*, North Holland, 1959.
Thomas, I. (trans.), *Greek Mathematical Works*, Loeb Classical Library, 1967.
Thomson, James, 'What the Tortoise should have said to Achilles', *Ratio*, 1973.
van Heijenoort, J. (ed.), *From Frege to Gödel: A Source Book in Mathematical Logic*, Harvard University Press, 1971.
Wang, Hao, 'A survey of Skolem's work in logic', in T. Skolem (1970).
From Mathematics to Philosophy, Routledge and Kegan Paul, 1974.
Wittgenstein, L., *Remarks on the Foundations of Mathematics*, Basil Blackwell, 1956.

Wright, Crispin, 'Language-mastery and the Sorites paradox', in Gareth Evans and John McDowell (1976).

Zermelo, E., 'Proof that every set can be well ordered', in van Heijenoort (1971).

'A new proof of the possibility of a well ordering', in van Heijenoort (1971).

General Index

INDEX LOCORUM